PRICEWATERHOUSECOOPERS

Guide to
the New Tax Law

Richard J. Berry Jr.,
M.B.A., C.P.A., D.B.A.

Michael B. Kennedy,
M.B.A., C.P.A.

and Bernard S. Kent,
J.D., C.P.A., P.F.S.

Ballantine Books
New York

Contents

CONTENTS

YEAR-ROUND TAX PLANNING STRATEGIES

CONTENTS

YEAR-END TAX SAVING STRATEGIES

Contents

A NUTS-AND-BOLTS REVIEW

ACKNOWLEDGMENTS

A publication of this kind does not come together without the invaluable contributions of many. In particular, we would like to thank Editorial Director Mark Friedlich for his outstanding efforts toward making this book a success.

We also express gratitude to the many partners and professionals of PricewaterhouseCoopers LLP who have spent a significant portion of their careers working with clients to develop strategies designed to help build, preserve, and maximize wealth.

RICHARD J. BERRY JR.
Partner, Tax and Legal Services Americas Theater Leader

MICHAEL B. KENNEDY
Partner, National Director of Personal Financial Services

BERNARD S. KENT
Partner, Midwest Region Director of Personal Financial Services

Introduction

The hardest thing in the world to understand, Albert Einstein once noted, is the income tax. And that was 60 years ago. Since then, the U.S. Tax Code has become ever more intricate. President Ronald Reagan's tax "simplification" in 1986 quickly bred new layers of complexity, and the recently enacted Economic Growth and Tax Relief Reconciliation Act of 2001 promises to keep changing the Code in installments for a decade to come.

When President George W. Bush signed the bill into law, he hailed it as the deepest tax cut in two decades. This reform, he said, would slash tax rates, kill off the "death tax" and the "marriage penalty," and bestow benefits ranging from tax-free education savings to expanded retirement accounts.

Of course, there is much more to the Tax Relief Act than meets the eye. Many of its benefits, including the end of estate taxes and relief from the marriage penalty, won't take effect for years. Other provisions, such as a new deduction for college costs and relief for middle-class taxpayers from the Alternative Minimum Tax (AMT), will be phased in early only to disappear within a few years. In fact, the whole structure of what was done by the Tax Act vanishes unless Congress changes its mind before the end of 2010. The law's sunset provision will end all the reforms and put the old Tax Code back in place in 2011.

In effect, this guarantees a decade of change in every citizen's financial life. And since the changes in the tax law are dynamic—they will be phased in over the next decade, some elements taking effect now, some in subsequent years—careful planning by taxpayers is more important than ever. It will allow prudent taxpayers to time their activities to take full advantage of the law's changes. Income, tax payments, and charitable contributions, for example, may be accelerated or deferred to coincide with provisions of the law as they phase in or out.

In truth, taxes and their implications reach into every aspect of our personal finances, from deciding where to live to the education of our children to our investment strategies and retirement planning. It is no exaggeration, in fact, to say that financial life begins with taxes. And Mr. Einstein's comment notwithstanding, the Tax Code really can be understood. Moreover, we owe it to ourselves and to our families to make the effort.

As signed by President Bush, the new law affects four major areas of the Tax Code: individual income tax rate reductions, increased child credits, marriage penalty relief, and estate tax relief. It also provides tax assistance for education-related costs, encourages personal savings through expanded Individual Retirement Accounts (IRAs), and creates broad pension reform.

The largest share of the tax reduction—fully 65 percent—comes from lower marginal income tax rates for individuals. Child-related items account for 13 percent of the cuts, and phasing out the estate tax takes another 10 percent, leaving only a total of 12 percent for reducing the marriage penalty, pension and IRA reform, education incentives, and relief from the AMT.

To hold the estimated cost of the new law to $1.35 trillion over 10 years, Congress decreed that many of the tax cuts and other improvements occur in later years or apply only temporarily. For example, relief from the AMT is limited, and actually ends after 2004; marriage penalty relief doesn't begin until 2005; and full estate tax repeal doesn't occur until 2010.

Much has been made of the law's sunset provision, which cancels the new law entirely after December 31, 2010. This clause was included in the Tax Act to comply with complex congressional budget rules, and it would restore all the tax rules and rates that were in effect before the 2001 Tax Act was enacted. In the end, however, while Congress is likely to change many provisions of the Act over the next 10 years, it is highly unlikely that the massive tax increase now scheduled for January 1, 2011, will actually occur.

This book will spell out the most important features of the new law and explain the opportunities it offers taxpayers to seize new advantages and plan for the coming changes. In the process, the book will explain how taxpayers can use these advantages to reduce their tax payments—as well as what to look for in the years ahead.

Who We Are

We are personal financial services professionals at PricewaterhouseCoopers (http://www.pwcglobal.com), one of the leading worldwide organizations of tax advisers, management consultants, and accountants and auditors. The firm operates in more than 150 countries and territories, advising large and small businesses, individuals, governments, and nonprofit organizations.

More than 300 personal financial services professionals in the United States provide high-net-worth individuals with comprehensive financial planning services including estate and gift tax planning, income tax consulting and preparation, compensation and stock option planning, investment advisory services, retirement planning, and charitable giving strategies.

How to Use This Book

Chapter by chapter, we clarify the vital sections of the new tax law, with concrete examples that tell taxpayers what they need to know to build a solid base for planning and then to begin to map their own dollar-saving strategies. Remember, however, that oversimplification is dangerous. We strongly recommend that taxpayers understand at least the basic provisions of the law and the fundamentals of the Tax Code before planning, say, educational savings or stock option strategy—that is why we wrote this book. Please keep in mind that this book covers federal tax law and rules with some discussion of state law. It is important that you review appropriate state and local tax law and rules before implementing tax planning strategies.

Here's what lies ahead:

- Chapter 1 spells out the key elements of the new Tax Act, explaining briefly what each major provision does, how it works, and its timing.
- The law's impact on investments and stock options is the subject of Chapter 2. Timing will be crucial in this area as various provisions of the law phase in and out.
- Retirement planning should be part of every taxpayer's strategy from the time he or she begins working. Chapter 3 discusses how to make planning for retirement a reality in light of the new law.
- The tax advantages of home ownership have been received-wisdom for decades. But Chapter 4 explores the subtle differences the new law will make when it comes to owning a home.

- The tax bill provides incentives for education, with specific provisions affecting primary, secondary, and higher institutions. Chapter 5 covers how to maximize savings for education.
- How can you structure your estate for a time when the death tax is gradually phasing out, only to reappear after 10 years? Chapter 6 offers estate planning ideas.
- Chapter 7 sums up important strategies for year-end tax planning in a quick planning guide.
- When preparing your taxes, moving deductions to the previous tax year can save significant dollars. Chapter 8 describes those deductions which may be best to accelerate.
- Chapter 9 applies the same year-end tax saving principles to deferring income from one year to the next, when it may be taxed less under the new Act.
- Chapter 10 explains basic tax concepts as they have evolved in the Tax Code and puts the 2001 changes into context.

Throughout each chapter there are a number of special features. Much of the text consists of individual "Observations"—brief, clear explanations of specific features of the new law and how they will be applied. There are also occasional passages labeled "Caution," which warn of possible blunders taxpayers might make based on a misinterpretation of the law. In addition, each chapter contains an "Idea Checklist" that offers readers a quick summary of concepts to be used for taking advantage of the new law and its changes.

Let's Get Started

It is human, and normal, to be intimidated by the subject of taxes. Back in the 1920s, we are told, the great writer Joseph Conrad received an official-looking envelope, delivered to his London home. He left it unopened on his desk for several weeks. He was afraid, he explained later: "I thought it was a tax notice." Only after the British government dispatched a messenger to Conrad's house did he discover that the envelope contained an offer of knighthood.

For most of us, our dealings with the Internal Revenue Service won't end with a royal tap on the shoulder, but we can benefit greatly if we take the initiative and make the effort to overcome such fears. When it comes to taxes, forewarned is forearmed. An investment of time and effort in forming a strategy for the coming years will pay off, year after year.

THE ECONOMIC GROWTH AND TAX RELIEF RECONCILIATION ACT OF 2001

The New Law's Key Provisions

The mood was quietly jubilant in the East Room of the White House as President George W. Bush signed the $1.35 trillion tax cut of 2001. While a Marine Corps band played "Hail to the Chief," the president used a different pen to write each letter of his name, then handed the pens to the key Republican and Democratic legislators whose support had turned the bill into law.

"Across-the-board tax relief does not happen often in Washington, D.C.," the president said. "In fact, since World War II, it has happened only twice: President Kennedy's tax cut in the sixties and President Reagan's tax cuts in the 1980s. And now it's happening for the third time, and it's about time."

Celebration was surely in order: Any tax relief is welcome. Yet the Economic Growth and Tax Relief Reconciliation Act of 2001 was more than a tax cut. It was a huge and complex changing-of-the-rules of the economic game. For informed citizens, the Tax Act of 2001 offers opportunities to plan for the changes due to occur in the next decade. They can take advantage of each provision as it phases in (and sometimes phases out), adjusting their investments and accelerating (moving into an earlier year) or deferring (delaying to the following year) their income and deductions to keep the greatest possible share of income for themselves and their families.

For such taxpayers, the new law may affect their entire economic lives. It will surely alter the way they invest their money, the way they save for their children's education and their own retirement, and the way they write their wills and structure their estates.

Their first step, however, must be to achieve an understanding of the coming changes and how they will work. This book aims to make that task as painless as possible. In this chapter we will begin by discussing the law's provisions in each of four main areas:

1. Rate Reductions, Tax Credits, and Deductions

All taxpayers will benefit from a new 10 percent bracket, which was carved out of the old 15 percent bracket. For married couples, the new tax rate applies to the first $12,000 of taxable income and will save them as much as $600 a year. In higher brackets, tax rates will fall in stages over the next five years. The top rate of 39.6 percent, paid by the top 1 percent of taxpayers, will fall to 35 percent; the 36 percent rate to 33 percent; the 31 percent rate to 28 percent; and the 28 percent rate to 25 percent. The child credit will rise in increments to $1,000, and the credit for child care expenses will also increase. Limits on personal exemptions and itemized deductions, which were formerly imposed in stages as income rose, will be phased out by 2010. There will be limited relief from the Alternative Minimum Tax (AMT), although this relief will not apply after 2004. And married people who pay more tax than they would as singles will get some relief, beginning in 2005.

2. Education Reforms

In 2002, the maximum contribution that can be made to an educational Individual Retirement Account (IRA), now called a Coverdell Education Savings Account, will quadruple to $2,000 in after-tax money. Income from these accounts can be withdrawn tax-free to pay for school expenses, including tuition for private and parochial schools and expenses for state-approved homeschooling, as well as for college. The so-called Section 529 plan, for parents saving for tuition and expenses at colleges and universities, will expand to include plans of private institutions. Congress also increased the deductibility of interest on student loans and created a short-lived deduction for up to $4,000 in college tuition for couples earning less than $130,000.

3. Retirement Plan Changes

The law provides major new incentives for retirement savings. The Roth IRA, which is funded with after-tax money and offers tax-free withdrawal of gains, will be extended to some high-income families who did not previously qualify, and the limits on contributions will be raised. Limits on annual funding for conventional IRAs will be phased up from $2,000 to $5,000 in 2008, and contributions to 401(k) and equivalent plans will phase up to a maximum of $15,000 in 2006. Workers who are age 50 or older will be allowed to make larger contributions, and there are special tax credits to help low-income taxpayers save for retirement.

4. Estate Tax Changes

Reforms of the so-called death tax have created considerable estate planning complexities for the wealthiest 2 percent of taxpayers—those who may owe taxes on their accumulated wealth when they die. The amount exempt from being taxed will keep rising and the top rate will keep falling until the tax phases out entirely in 2010. On the other hand, unless Congress intervenes, the tax will come back in 2011, just as it was in 2001. And even if this revival is later repealed, new rules will require heirs to pay tax on some of the capital gains from their inherited wealth.

We will now take up these changes, and what they portend for individual taxpayers, in more detail.

Rate Reductions, Tax Credits, and Deductions

The 2001 Tax Act contains the largest tax rate reductions since Ronald Reagan was president. Unfortunately, individuals will not immediately benefit from the cuts. Beginning in 2001, the cuts will be phased in over five years and will not take full effect until 2006 at the earliest.

New 10 Percent Income Tax Bracket

The 2001 Tax Act created a new 10 percent income tax rate out of the lowest part of the 15 percent bracket, beginning in 2001. For 2001, however, most people will realize the benefit from this rate in the form of a rebate check by the end of 2001. The 10 percent bracket will apply to:

• The first $6,000 of taxable income for single individuals ($7,000 beginning in 2008).
• The first $10,000 of taxable income for heads of households.
• The first $12,000 for married couples filing joint returns ($14,000 beginning in 2008).

Observation: Everyone who pays regular income tax, not just those in low-income brackets, will benefit from the new 10 percent category.

Advance Payment Checks

Generally, an individual taxpayer who filed a return, paid income tax for 2000, and was neither a dependent of another taxpayer nor a nonresident alien, will get the benefit of the 10 percent bracket by way of an advance-payment check from the U.S. Treasury Department by October 2001. The maximum advance payment will be $300 for unmarried people, $500 for heads of households, and $600 for married taxpayers filing jointly.

Those who do not qualify for this full payment (because in 2000, they either did not owe enough tax or were dependents) may be entitled to a credit on their 2001 returns. The amount will be equal to 5 percent of the amount of income that otherwise would qualify for the new 10 percent income tax rate, less the amount of any advance payment received during 2001. Thus, the maximum "rate reduction credit," which will be computed on the 2001 return, will also be $300 for single taxpayers, $500 for heads of households, and $600 for married taxpayers filing jointly.

The taxpayer will reconcile the amount of the credit and rebate check when he or she files 2001 returns, and will do so by:

1. Completing a worksheet calculating the amount of the credit based on his or her 2001 tax return.
2. Subtracting from the credit the amount of the received check.

Most taxpayers will receive the full check in 2001 and won't be entitled to any credit on their 2001 return. If your advance payment, which is based on your 2000 tax return situation, turns out to be more than you would have been entitled to based on your 2001 tax circumstances, you don't have to repay the difference.

Reminder: You do not have to report the amount of the advance-payment check you receive as income on your 2001 income tax return.

Reduction in 28 Percent and Higher Tax Rates

The 2001 Tax Act gradually reduces the previous income tax rates of 28 percent, 31 percent, 36 percent, and 39.6 percent to 25 percent, 28 percent, 33 percent, and 35 percent, respectively, beginning July 1, 2001. For 2001, individual tax rates higher than 15 percent are effectively cut by 0.5 percent. The table that follows shows the scheduled regular income tax rate reductions.

Calendar Year	28% rate reduced to:	31% rate reduced to:	36% rate reduced to:	39.6% rate reduced to:
2001	27.5%	30.5%	35.5%	39.1%
2002–2003	27%	30%	35%	38.6%
2004–2005	26%	29%	34%	37.6%
2006 and later	25%	28%	33%	35%

Observation: Although, technically, individual tax rates were reduced as of July 1, 2001, the preceding table reflects the fact that income earned in the second half of 2001 is not subject to a rate lower than the one set for income earned in the first half. Rather, a "blended" rate applies for all of 2001, so that each rate above 15 percent will drop by one-half of 1 percent for the entire year.

Observation: Since rates will be dropping each year, taxpayers should consider deferring ordinary income until later tax years. For example, it might be wise to postpone exercising certain stock options and to delay year-end bonuses and other lump-sum payments until the following January.

Other options to consider include taking itemized deductions (such as charitable contributions, which are discussed below) in earlier, higher-tax years. For example, it may be wise to make charitable contributions at the end of 2001 that ordinarily would be made early in 2002. Or, one might make deductible state estimated tax payments in December rather than in January. (Note: There are some limitations on deferring income or accelerating deductions.)

Caution: One must also consider the effects of deferring income or accelerating deductions on your Alternative Minimum Tax (AMT) position.

 Observation: Taxpayers who anticipate making charitable contributions over the course of the next several years should consider making contributions while still in higher tax brackets, unless the current tax benefit from itemized deductions is minimal because of the income level. If you wish to take a deduction now for your gifts to be paid to charities in the future, you can contribute to a donor-advised philanthropic fund, private foundation, or other charitable vehicles.

Observation: Generally, the reduction in marginal rates, particularly the creation of the 10 percent income tax bracket, enhances the tax advantage of moving income over to children age 14 and older. When the new rates are entirely phased in, people in the top income bracket, for example, can save 25 percent in taxes by shifting up to $6,000 in income to a child. That is the difference between the 10 percent bracket and what will be the top 35 percent bracket. (Be careful about this, however, because the unearned income of children *under* age 14 is usually taxed under the so-called kiddie tax rules at the parents' marginal tax rate.)

Observation: By 2006, when the reduction in marginal rates is scheduled to be fully effective, the gap between long-term capital gains and ordinary income tax rates will be reduced (assuming the capital gains rate is not lowered by future tax legislation). This, in turn, should translate into fewer transactions being timed specifically around capital gains considerations or fewer transactions altogether.

Observation: It may be possible to reduce estimated tax payments to reflect lower rates. The IRS has released revised withholding tables for wages paid after June 30, 2001. On the other hand, you may need to increase your estimated tax payments in order to have a safe estimate, because your withholding for the year may now be less than last year's withholding.

Observation: The reduction in marginal rates makes tax-exempt investments, such as municipal bonds, relatively less attractive unless and until those investments match the reduction with higher yields.

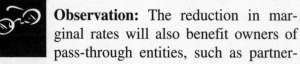 **Observation:** The reduction in marginal rates will also benefit owners of pass-through entities, such as partnerships, limited liability companies, and S corporations, each of which subjects its owner to only one level of individual taxation.

Upper-Income Individuals Won't Lose Deductions

After 2005, the 2001 Tax Act phases out the overall limitation on itemized deductions, which now reduces the value of certain itemized deductions claimed by higher-income individuals. In effect, these higher-income individuals will have an even greater rate reduction.

Now, in 2001, itemized deductions—except medical expenses; casualty, theft, or gambling losses; and investment interest expense—are reduced by 3 percent of the individual's adjusted gross income (AGI) above $132,950 for unmarried people as well as married couples filing joint returns ($66,475 for married individuals filing separately). Although these amounts are adjusted annually for inflation, this rule can cause one to lose as much as 80 percent of deductions in this category.

The 2001 Tax Act phases out this limitation by reducing it by one-third for 2006 and 2007, two-thirds for 2008 and 2009, and eliminating it altogether after 2009.

Personal Exemptions Won't Be Lost

The 2001 Tax Act also phases out the restrictions on personal exemptions that are now imposed on higher-income taxpayers. Beginning after 2005, those affected will receive what is, in effect, an additional tax rate reduction.

Currently, deductions for personal exemptions ($2,900 each in 2001) are reduced or eliminated at higher income levels. For 2001, the deduction must be reduced by 2 percent for each $2,500 ($1,250 for married people filing separately) or a portion of $2,500 that the taxpayer's AGI exceeds $199,450 for joint returns; $99,725 for married couples filing separately; $166,200 for heads of households; and $132,950 for single individuals. For 2001, personal exemptions are completely phased out at $321,950 on joint returns; $160,975 for married individuals filing separate returns; $288,700 for heads of households; and $255,450 for single individuals (see Chapter 10 for 2002 figures).

Under the 2001 Tax Act, the personal exemption phase-out will be reduced by one-third for 2006 and 2007; two-thirds for 2008 and 2009; and eliminated altogether after that.

Marriage Penalty Relief

The 2001 Tax Act helps reduce the marriage penalty that wedded couples are subject to. However, relief does not start until 2005 and is not fully phased in until 2009.

The relief takes the following two forms:

1. Standard Deduction Increase. The basic standard deduction for married couples filing joint returns will gradually increase until it is twice the standard deduction for single filers. (In 2005, the standard deduction for joint filers will be 174 percent of that for singles, and will increase each year until it reaches 200 percent in 2009.) Starting in 2005, the standard deduction for married taxpayers who file separately will be equal to that for singles.

Observation: Married couples who itemize their deductions will not benefit from this change if their itemized deductions already exceed twice the standard deduction amount for single filers.

2. Expansion of the 15 Percent Bracket. The 15 percent income tax bracket for married couples filing joint returns will gradually grow to twice the size of the 15 percent bracket for single filers. Beginning in 2005, this increase will be fully phased in by 2008.

Observation: Unlike the change in the standard deduction, which will only benefit people who do not itemize, the expansion of the 15 percent tax bracket will help all married couples with taxable income in this or higher brackets as long as they are not subject to Alternative Minimum Tax. The reason is that more of their income will be taxed at a lower rate.

The Bottom Line

Putting together all of the tax reductions discussed thus far, how much can an individual expect to save year by year? To answer that, let's look at a married couple who files jointly, has two dependent children, $500,000 of ordinary income (wages, interest, and dividends), and $50,000 of itemized deductions. Here's how much they would save in 2001, 2006, and 2010:

Year	Tax	Savings Over Prior Law
2001–Prior law	$154,378	$0
2001–2001 Tax Act	$151,703	$2,675
2006–Reduction in marginal rates fully phased in	$134,710	$16,993
2010–Elimination of phase-out of itemized deductions/personal exemptions	$122,465	$31,913

Child Tax Credit

A taxpayer with dependent children younger than age 17 is now entitled to a child tax credit of $500 per child; however, the credit begins to phase out once the modified AGI (adjusted gross income with some adjustments that do not affect most taxpayers) reaches $110,000 on a joint return ($75,000 for single individuals or heads of households, and $55,000 for married couples filing separately). In general, the child tax credit is nonrefundable, which means that a refund is not issued if its total exceeds the tax owed. (More will be said about refundable credits shortly.) However, for lower-income families with three or more qualifying children under age 17, the credit is refundable for the amount that their Social Security taxes surpass their earned income credit.

The 2001 Tax Act gradually increases the child

credit to $1,000 over 10 years, which is represented in the following table:

Calendar Year	Credit Amount Per Child
2001–2004	$600
2005–2008	$700
2009	$800
2010	$1,000

In addition, the child credit is now refundable up to 10 percent of a taxpayer's earned income in excess of $10,000 for calendar years 2001 to 2004 (the $10,000 amount is indexed for inflation beginning in 2002). The percentage increases from 10 to 15 percent starting in 2005. A refundable tax credit is one that results in a refund if the credit exceeds the amount of tax owed. For families with three or more children, the credit, which remains refundable, is available if it brings a larger refund than what would be received under the new rules. Also, the child credit will be allowed permanently against the Alternative Minimum Tax.

Adoption Credit

Currently, individual taxpayers may claim a credit of up to $5,000 per child ($6,000 for a child with special needs) for certain expenses associated with adopting a child. Employees can receive and pay no income taxes on a maximum of $5,000 for qualified adoption expenses paid by their employers.

Both the credit and exclusion phase out at modified AGI levels between $75,000 and $115,000. The exclusion and the credit for children, other than those with special needs, are scheduled to expire after 2001.

The 2001 Tax Act:

- Makes the adoption credit and the exclusion for adoption expenses permanent.
- Increases the credit and the exclusion to $10,000 per child beginning in 2002.
- Beginning in 2002, increases the phase-out range to modified AGI levels between $150,000 and $190,000.
- Beginning in 2003, allows the full $10,000 credit for special-needs adoptions to be claimed in the year the adoption is finalized, regardless of the amount of actual expenses.

 Reminder: The adoption credit can be claimed permanently against the Alternative Minimum Tax.

Dependent Care Credit

Currently, a credit is allowed for certain dependent care expenses that enables parents to work. For most people (those with an AGI over $28,000), this credit amounts to 20 percent of $2,400 (maximum) of incurred expenses ($4,800 for two or more qualifying children under age 13 or older dependents who are incapable of caring for themselves). Thus, an individual with two qualifying children is generally limited to a credit of $960. Those with lower incomes are eligible for this credit at a rate as high as 30 percent of incurred expenses.

Beginning in 2003, the 2001 Tax Act raises the amount of expenses eligible for credit under "dependent care" to $3,000 ($6,000 for two or more qualifying children or dependents).

The maximum credit rate is also increased from 30 percent to 35 percent, and will phase down more slowly than under the previous rules. For example, after 2002, an individual with two qualifying children and an AGI of $29,000 will be entitled to a maximum credit of $1,680 (28 percent of $6,000). Taxpayers with two or more qualifying children or dependents and income over $43,000 will be entitled to a maximum credit of $1,200 (20 percent of $6,000).

Alternative Minimum Tax

The Alternative Minimum Tax, or AMT, was intended to ensure that high-income taxpayers who benefit from various deductions, credits, and exemptions pay at least a minimum amount of tax. The AMT is calculated by reducing or eliminating the tax benefits that have been claimed for regular income tax purposes. Next, the exemption amount is subtracted, and the AMT tax rates are applied to the balance. The taxpayer then compares the result with his or her regular tax and pays the higher amount.

The AMT exemption is available for taxpayers with relatively modest incomes. In 2000, $45,000 was the total amount allowed for married couples filing joint returns ($33,750 for single taxpayers, and $22,500 for married individuals filing separately). Phased out for higher-income taxpayers, the AMT exemption amount has not kept pace with inflation, making it less protective for a growing number of middle-income taxpayers.

The 2001 Tax Act raises the amounts of the AMT exemption by $4,000 to $49,000 for married couples filing jointly, and by $2,000 to $35,750 for single taxpayers and $24,500 for married individuals filing separately. However, these increases apply only from 2001 through 2004. The AMT tax rates remain at 26 percent for the first $175,000 of AMT income ($87,500 for married individuals filing separately) after the exemption, and 28 percent for the balance. The 2001 Tax Act did not alter the phase-out of the AMT exemption amount for higher incomes.

Observation: Although the AMT exemption has been increased slightly, taxpayers subject to the AMT may not realize the reductions in the regular income tax rates. Furthermore, the rate reductions themselves will increase many people's exposure to the AMT.

Example: A married couple with two dependent children has a combined income of $200,000; together, they have $45,000 of itemized deductions ($30,000 for mortgage interest, $5,000 for property tax, and $10,000 for state income tax). Before the 2001 Tax Act changes, this couple would have owed approximately

$33,700 in income taxes and no AMT. After the regular tax rate reduction takes full effect in 2006, that income tax would drop to approximately $28,750. However, because the increase in the AMT exemption expires in 2005 and regular taxes become substantially lower in 2006, they would pay $5,040 in AMT in addition to the $28,750 of regular tax.

Education Reforms

The 2001 Tax Act provides improved tax incentives that make education at all levels more affordable. These are the major enhancements:

- Increased limits on contributions to Education IRAs.
- Tax-free withdrawals from Section 529 programs will be allowed.
- Employer-provided graduate education assistance.
- Expansion of the student loan interest deduction.
- New tax deduction for college costs.

 Caution: All of these changes are scheduled to lapse after 2010 unless Congress intervenes to extend them.

Education IRAs

For 2001, annual contributions to an Education IRA (now officially called a Coverdell Education Savings Account) for a specific beneficiary could not exceed a total of $500 total from all donors. The $500 limit is phased out for individuals with an AGI over $95,000, and for married couples filing jointly with an AGI over $150,000. Distributions are tax-free up to the amount of the beneficiary's qualified higher-education expenses in the year of distribution. A portion of distributions that exceed those expenses in any given year is taxable and subject to a 10 percent penalty.

Under the 2001 Tax Act, the annual limit on contributions to Coverdell Education Savings Accounts will increase to $2,000 per child beginning in 2002. The contribution limit for married couples filing jointly will begin to phase out at $190,000, which is twice the limit for single taxpayers. Also, corporations and tax-exempt organizations, among other entities, may contribute to Coverdell Education Savings Accounts regardless of their income as long as they adhere to the limit of $2,000 per beneficiary.

Also starting in 2002, kindergarten, elementary-, and secondary-school expenses (public, private, or religious) as well as certain after-school programs will qualify as education expenses that are eligible for tax-free treatment. Computer equipment, software, and Internet access will also be included in this category.

Other improvements for Coverdell Education Savings Accounts starting in 2002 are:

• A HOPE Scholarship credit or a Lifetime Learning credit may be claimed in the same year that a

tax-free distribution is taken from a Coverdell Education Savings Account, as long as the same expenses aren't used to claim both the exclusion and a credit.
• Contributions may be made to both a Coverdell Education Savings Account and to a qualified tuition program in the same year for the same beneficiary without incurring an excise tax that applies before 2002.

Observation: Parents should consider whether Coverdell Education Savings Accounts or Section 529 programs will affect their chances of receiving financial aid for college (see Chapter 5).

Section 529 Qualified Tuition Programs

State-sponsored college savings plans allow tuition credits to be purchased or contributions to be made to college savings accounts on behalf of a designated beneficiary who is taxed when the tuition credit is distributed or received to the extent that it exceeds what was contributed on his or her behalf. Contributors are taxed on any refund from the program that exceeds the contributions made for a beneficiary.

Under the 2001 Tax Act, private educational institutions will be able to establish plans like those of many states. In the private plans, a person will purchase tuition certificates or credits, but a college savings account will not be available.

The biggest change made to qualified tuition plans is that distributions from a Section 529 qualified state tuition plan, if used to pay for qualified higher-education costs, will be tax-free starting in 2002. After 2003, this tax-free treatment also will apply to distributions made from private qualified tuition programs.

In addition, starting in 2002, rollovers may be made from one plan to another once every 12 months without tax consequences, even if the beneficiary stays the same. The present rule that allows transfers between qualified accounts for different beneficiaries in the same family will be expanded to include transfers that will benefit a first cousin of the original beneficiary.

Observation: This modification will enable grandparents to switch beneficiaries among their grandchildren.

The HOPE Scholarship credit and the Lifetime Learning credit may be claimed in the same year that a distribution is taken from a qualified tuition plan, but the credit and the exclusion can't both result from the same expenses.

Employer Education Assistance

Currently, an employer can pay a maximum of $5,250 per year of educational expenses on behalf of an employee, under an education-assistance plan that allows that income to be tax-free to the employee, and exempt from payroll taxes. These benefits were scheduled to expire for any course that began after 2001. And they were not available at all for graduate courses.

The 2001 Tax Act, however, extends the exclusion to graduate courses beginning after 2001 and, in addition, makes the exclusion (for both undergraduate and graduate courses) permanent.

Observation: Even without this specific tax break, reimbursements by employers for job-related courses, which are those that maintain or improve a skill currently used in the recipient's trade or business or are required to continue his or her employment, are tax-free. This does not include courses that lead to a new profession.

Student Loan Interest Deduction

Currently, taxpayers may deduct up to $2,500 annually for interest paid on qualified education loans for the first 60 months of the repayment period when interest payments are required. The maximum deduction phases out for single taxpayers with an AGI between $40,000 and $55,000, and for married taxpayers filing jointly with an AGI between $60,000 and $75,000.

Starting in 2002, the 2001 Tax Act repeals the 60-month limit during which qualified student loan interest is deductible. It also increases the phase-out range to $50,000 to $65,000 of AGI for single taxpayers, and $100,000 to $130,000 for married couples filing jointly. The phase-out thresholds will be adjusted for inflation after 2002.

Deduction for Qualified Higher-Education Expenses

Although many tax breaks for education savings and expenditures currently exist, no general deduction for tuition expenses not related to one's job is available. The 2001 Tax Act changes that by providing a deduction for a limited amount of qualified higher-education expenses paid on behalf of oneself or one's spouse or dependents. The benefit extends to people who itemize deductions as well as to those who claim the standard deduction.

Only a taxpayer with relatively modest income can claim the new deduction. In 2002 and 2003, the maximum deduction has been set at $3,000, and can be claimed only if the AGI is $65,000 or less, or $130,000 for married couples filing joint returns.

In 2004 and 2005, the maximum deduction increases to $4,000 for those with an AGI of $65,000 ($130,000 for married couples filing jointly) or less. A maximum deduction of $2,000 is available if one's AGI is more than $65,000, but not more than $80,000 (between $130,000 and $160,000 for married couples filing jointly).

The disadvantages to the new deduction include: it will not be available after 2005, and it cannot be claimed in the same year as a HOPE Scholarship credit or a Lifetime Learning credit for the same student. Finally, taxpayers cannot deduct expenses that were taken into account when determining the amount of a Coverdell Educations Savings Account or a qualified tax-free tuition plan distribution.

Highlights of Major Education Changes

Highlights	Old Law	New Law
Education IRAs (Coverdell Education Savings Accounts)		
Contribution limit	$500	$2,000
AGI phase-out (single/joint)	$95,000/$150,000	$95,000/$190,000
Qualified expenses	higher education only	elementary, secondary, and higher education
Section 529 plans		
Earnings used for education	taxable	tax-free
Employer assistance programs		
Eligible coursework	undergraduate courses only	undergraduate and postgraduate courses
Student loan interest deduction		
Interest payments eligible	first 60 months of payments	no limit
AGI phase-out (single/joint)	$40,000/$60,000	$50,000/$100,000

Retirement Plan Changes

The 2001 Tax Act increases the overall limit on amounts that may be added annually to defined contribution plans by employers, and employees including 401(k) plans and profit sharing plans, beginning with the 2002 plan year. The current limit is either $35,000 or 25 percent of compensation, depending on which total is lower. That limit will be raised to whichever is less—100 percent of compensation or $40,000. In the future, the dollar limit will be indexed for inflation in $1,000 increments.

Observation: The increase to 100 percent of compensation is intended to assist individuals whose working histories are interrupted in accumulating more retirement savings. While the increased limit applies to all plan participants, it is expected that second-income spouses will make the most use of it.

Caution: This change applies to the allocation limitation, not the deduction limitation.

Increase in Benefit Limit

The 2001 Tax Act increases the maximum annual benefit that a defined benefit pension plan can fund. It is raised from the current amount of $140,000 to $160,000, starting in 2002. The limit is reduced for benefits beginning before age 62 and is increased for benefit payments commencing after age 65.

403(b)/457 Changes

After 2001, the maximum exclusion allowance under tax-deferred 403(b) annuities is repealed and replaced with the 100 percent of compensation limit. In addition, the special alternative elections for certain 403(b) plans are repealed. The 33⅓ percent limit under 457 (state and local government employee) plans also is repealed and replaced with the 100 percent of compensation limit. The maximum dollar limit will be the same amount that applies to the 401(k) plans.

Vesting of Employer Contributions

The 2001 Tax Act increased many tax incentives for retirement savings, although several are optional, not mandatory. They allow, but don't require, employers with qualified retirement plans to adopt the changes. However, one favorable change for employees is mandatory: faster vesting of employer-matching contributions.

For plan years beginning after 2001, employer-matching contributions made under a qualified retirement plan or a 403(b) annuity must vest (i.e., cannot be forfeited) either 100 percent after three years or 20 percent per year, beginning with the second year of service and increasing to 100 percent after six years of service. The new vesting schedule applies only to employees who have some service after the 2000 plan year. These rules will also apply to collectively bargained plans in later years.

Caution: The new, more liberal vesting requirements do not apply to nonmatching employer contributions. And, remaining unchanged, individuals' own plan contributions are 100 percent vested at all times.

Increased Compensation Limit

Beginning in 2002, the 2001 Tax Act increases the amount of compensation that can be taken into account for retirement plan purposes from $170,000 to $200,000. This means that larger contributions and benefits are possible for those with relatively high compensation. The $200,000 compensation limit will be indexed for inflation in multiples of $5,000.

Increased 401(k) and SIMPLE Plan Deferrals

The 2001 Tax Act increases the amount of salary that employees can contribute to a 401(k) plan. These provisions also apply to 403(b) annuities and 457 deferred compensation arrangements. For 2002, up to $11,000 or 100 percent of compensation—whichever is less—can be deferred to a 401(k) plan account, after which the dollar limit on annual deferrals will increase in $1,000 increments until it reaches $15,000 in 2006.

The annual deferral limit for SIMPLE (savings incentive match plan for employees) plans that allow deferrals will increase to $7,000 in 2002, with $1,000 annual increases thereafter until it reaches $10,000 in 2005.

All of these deferral limits will be indexed annually in $500 increments after the increases are fully phased in.

Year	401(k) maximum deferral amount* if age is less than 50	SIMPLE maximum deferral amount* if age is less than 50
2001	$10,500	$6,500
2002	$11,000	$7,000
2003	$12,000	$8,000
2004	$13,000	$9,000
2005	$14,000	$10,000
2006 and later	$15,000 as indexed	$10,000 as indexed

* Cannot exceed 100% of compensation

Caution: A highly compensated employee (HCE) may not be allowed to take full advantage of the increased deferral limits after the 401(k) nondiscrimination tests are applied.

"Catch-Up" 401(k) and SIMPLE Plan Deferrals

Starting in 2002, taxpayers can elect to make additional pretax deferrals if they are 50 years of age or older. These catch-up amounts are: $1,000 in 2002; $2,000 in 2003; $3,000 in 2004; $4,000 in 2005; and $5,000 in 2006 and thereafter. The additional catch-up amount allowed under a SIMPLE plan is $500 for 2002, increasing by $500 each year until it reaches

$2,500 in 2006. The $5,000 and $2,500 amounts will be indexed for inflation after 2006.

The regular contribution limits and nondiscrimination rules will not apply to catch-up contributions, provided the plan permits all eligible participants to make them. Employers are generally permitted, but not required, to match catch-up contributions.

Year	401(k) maximum deferral amount* if at least age 50 (includes catch-up)	SIMPLE maximum deferral amount* if at least age 50 (includes catch-up)
2001	$10,500	$6,500
2002	$12,000	$7,500
2003	$14,000	$9,000
2004	$16,000	$10,500
2005	$18,000	$12,000
2006 and thereafter	$20,000 as indexed	$12,500 as indexed

* Cannot exceed 100% of compensation.

 Observation: Highly compensated employees and second-wage earners in families are more likely to have disposable income available to take advantage of the increases in the elective deferrals.

Observation: The allowance of extra contributions by employees age 50 or older should decrease the amount of corrective distributions to highly compensated employees and allow more of the executive's elective deferrals to remain in the plan. In addition, many executives otherwise limited under the plan will be able to take advantage of the catch-up provision and increase 401(k) elective deferrals without being either subjected to nondiscrimination tests or limited on the amounts of the annual additions.

Example: An executive who has more than $200,000 of compensation who defers the maximum under the current law will have an average deferral percentage (ADP) of 6.18 percent ($10,500/$170,000) for 2001. The maximum deferral for 2002 will produce an ADP of 5.5 percent. If the highly compensated employee is age 50, an additional $1,000 can be deferred, bringing the total deferral to $12,000 in 2002 without affecting the 5.5 percent ADP. A lower ADP will allow more of the executive's elective deferrals to remain in the plan.

403(b) and 457 Plans

The increased limits for elective deferrals, including the catch-ups, apply in general to 403(b) annuities and to 457 deferred compensation arrangements maintained by a state government employer. However, a catch-up contribution cannot be made to a 457 arrangement in the three years prior to retirement. But special rules that apply only to 457 plans allow the annual deferral to be increased to twice the applicable annual deferral. The rules that reduce the limits on contributions made to 457 plans by the amounts contributed to 403(b) and 401(k) plans are repealed, effective for years beginning after 2001. This change allows state government employers to increase retirement savings by making an elective deferral to a 457 plan and deferring the maximum amount to a 403(b) annuity or a 401(k) plan, as well.

Larger IRA Contributions

The 2001 Tax Act increases the maximum annual IRA contribution from $2,000, where it has remained static for nearly 20 years, to $3,000 for 2002 through 2004; $4,000 for 2005 through 2007; and $5,000 for 2008. The new contribution limit will be indexed annually for inflation after 2008 in $500 increments.

The 2001 Tax Act also permits extra catch-up contributions for those age 50 or older as of year-end.

Increased IRA Contribution Limits

Year	Regular IRA Contribution	Catch-Up Contribution
2002	$3,000	$500
2003	$3,000	$500
2004	$3,000	$500
2005	$4,000	$500
2006	$4,000	$1,000
2007	$4,000	$1,000
2008 and later	$5,000	$1,000

The maximum catch-up contributions are $500 from 2002 through 2005, and $1,000 after 2005.

Observation: These increases will give taxpayers and their spouses more opportunities to save for retirement so they can rely less on employer retirement plans and Social Security. Over long periods of time, even relatively modest additional savings will accumulate significantly.

Observation: The income limits for deductible IRAs, eligibility for Roth IRAs, and converting regular IRAs into Roth IRAs remain unchanged. As a result, the only benefit that higher-income taxpayers who are active participants in employer retirement plans (or whose spouses are) will realize from the IRA changes is the ability to make larger contributions to nondeductible regular IRAs.

New IRA/Employer Plan Combination

Enabling employees to save for retirement through payroll deductions, the 2001 Tax Act permits employers with qualified retirement plans or tax-sheltered annuities to create employer-sponsored IRAs as part of those plans. The new arrangement, which is called a Deemed IRA and will begin in 2003, must meet all the regular IRA requirements.

New Roth IRA/Employer Plan Combination

The 2001 Tax Act allows employees to designate elective deferrals (up to the dollar contribution limits discussed above) to 401(k) or 403(b) plans as Roth IRA contributions. This "Qualified Roth Contribution" program will be available as of 2006.

Even taxpayers whose incomes are too high to contribute to regular Roth IRAs can contribute to the new arrangements; the option will be available to all plan members. Thus, even high-income individuals can designate 401(k) deferrals as Roth IRA contributions if their plans are amended to permit it.

Designating elective deferrals as Roth IRA contributions converts the contributed amounts into after-tax, rather than pretax, contributions, which increases the up-front cost of saving in these vehicles. However, the Qualified Roth Contribution account must adhere to all of the regular Roth IRA rules regarding income tax on distributed earnings (not taxed if distributed after age 59½ and the Roth account has existed for five years), early distribution penalty, and rollovers.

Observation: Taxpayers will need to balance current and future advantages and disadvantages of elective deferrals or Roth IRA contributions each year, taking into account the time until distribution and the potential marginal tax bracket at distribution.

Rollovers

In general, the 2001 Tax Act expands one's ability to move funds from one type of retirement plan to another by allowing rollover contributions between regular retirement plans, such as 401(k) plans, tax-sheltered annuity plans (403(b) plans), and governmental retirement plans (Section 457 plans) beginning in 2002. After-tax contributions to employer plans are eligible to be rolled over beginning in 2002. Surviving spouse beneficiaries also will have more choices on rollover plans beginning in 2002.

Rollover Eligible Plans

Under current law, only IRAs and qualified plans can accept rollovers; the latter can accept rollovers only from other qualified plans or from "conduit" IRAs, and 403(b) plans can only accept rollovers from another 403(b) plan. The 2001 Tax Act expands the plans that can accept rollovers for distributions after 2001 to include 403(b) and 457 plans. Thus, any distributions from 401(k), 403(b), or 457 plans will be eligible to be rolled into any other plan. As was previously the case, a conduit IRA can be rolled into a qualified plan, 403(b) plan, or 457 plan, but only if it has not received any regular IRA contributions.

Observation: The current patchwork of rollover rules has been made a bit more consistent with these changes. The new rules are especially valuable for those who accept jobs with government or tax-exempt employers after working in the private sector.

 Caution: Any grandfathered features (eligibility for 10-year averaging; capital gains for pre-1974 accruals; or tax deferral on unrealized appreciation from distributed employer securities) may be lost in such a transfer. Thus, before rolling over funds from a tax-qualified plan, one should determine his or her continuing eligibility for special tax rules.

Rollover of After-Tax Contributions

For distributions made after 2001, the taxpayer can roll over after-tax contributions from employer plans to IRAs along with the taxable portion of the account at retirement. It will also be possible to roll over after-tax contributions into a new employer plan, provided it is a direct trustee-to-trustee transfer.

Rollovers of after-tax contributions must be accounted for separately. When they are distributed, special ordering rules apply for the after-tax account: earnings are deemed to be distributed first and contributions last.

Observation: Once an after-tax contribution is rolled over into an IRA, it cannot be rolled back into a qualified plan, 403(b) annuity, or 457 plan.

 Observation: For distributions before 2002, after-tax contributions cannot be rolled into IRA accounts or a different employer plan. The new, more liberal rules provide a significant benefit by increasing your ability to leave funds in tax deferred status after changing jobs.

The downside is that after-tax contributions add a layer of complexity. The rules for recovering after-tax contributions from IRA distributions differ from those for pension distributions. For example, under the 2001 Tax Act, a participant in a qualified plan who receives a distribution of $500,000 (including $200,000 in after-tax contributions) can roll over $300,000, keep the $200,000 of after-tax contributions, and pay no tax. However, an IRA owner in the same situation would be taxed on 60 percent of the $200,000 that wasn't rolled into an IRA.

Spousal Rollovers

Until now, a surviving spouse who is the beneficiary of a deceased employee's retirement plan could roll over the distribution only into an IRA. The 2001 Tax Act permits a rollover to the surviving spouse's own employer-sponsored plan. Thus, after 2001, a spouse can roll this sort of distribution into his or her own 401(k) plan or 403(b) tax-sheltered annuity.

Caution: Although this change permits the surviving spouse to consolidate funds in a single location, rolling into a qualified plan may not be the best approach because the beneficiary payout features of qualified plans are usually not as flexible as IRA payout features. The surviving spouse can preserve greater flexibility for payouts to beneficiaries by using an IRA rollover.

Tax Credit for Plan Contributions

For 2002 through 2006, a new nonrefundable tax credit is available to certain lower-income individuals who contribute to qualified retirement plans (including IRAs and Roth IRAs). This credit is in addition to any other deduction available. The maximum annual contribution eligible for the credit is $2,000.

The credit rate phases down from 50 percent to 10 percent of the contribution based on the individual's AGI. It is only available to those with an AGI below the beginning of the IRA deduction phase-out, and is totally phased out for those with an AGI above $50,000 for joint filers, $37,500 for head-of-household filers, and $25,000 for single filers. This credit is not available to students, taxpayers under age 18, or dependents.

Employer Provided Retirement Planning

The 2001 Tax Act stipulates that retirement planning services provided to employees and spouses are a nontaxable fringe benefit after 2001. Highly compensated employees qualify for this exclusion only if services are available on substantially similar terms to all employees who normally receive information regarding the employer's qualified plan. However, it is expected that employers will be able to limit the advice they offer to those at or near retirement age.

Before 2002, there is no specific exclusion for these services. However, many view general retirement planning information as a nontaxable fringe benefit as long as the discussions and illustrations are general and not particular to any single individual.

Caution: The exclusion is not available for other services associated with retirement planning such as tax preparation, legal, accounting, or brokerage services.

Observation: Retirement planning involves difficult income tax, investment, and logistic issues. Several professional groups participate in what has become a significant service industry, including accountants, attorneys, trust officers, financial planners, and brokers. The new exclusion should provide employees with greater access to these services.

Required Minimum Distributions

The Internal Revenue Service recently revamped and simplified its proposed regulations dealing with minimum distributions. The revised rules can be used by taxpayers beginning in 2001. The Act directs the IRS to revise the life-expectancy factors used to calculate minimum distributions. (The life-expectancy factors are from the original proposed regulations in the mid-1980s.)

 Observation: The IRS revisions to the proposed regulations thoroughly simplify what was a cluttered process. Congress had been examining IRA payout procedures with an eye toward simplifying them prior to the proposed regulation revisions. The 2001 Tax Act's directive to update the life-expectancy factors resulted from that process.

 Caution: A taxpayer who is going to receive a minimum required distribution from an IRA for 2001 should make sure it has been calculated using the revised proposed regulations. The revisions decrease by a ignificant degree the amount of required distributions for most people (see Chapter 3 for details).

Plan Loans to Owner-Employees

S corporation owners, partners, and sole proprietors will be able to borrow from their retirement plans without being liable for the "prohibited trans-actions" excise tax. This will be in effect beginning in 2002 provided the rules that apply to plan loans made to other participants are followed. Generally, this means the amounts that can be borrowed are limited to whichever is less: $50,000, or half the indi-vidual's account balance. Also, repayment with inter-est must be made at regular intervals over a term of no more than five years (longer for loans used to pur-chase a principal residence).

Small-Business Credit for Plan Start-Up Costs

To encourage small businesses to establish retire-ment plans for employees, the 2001 Tax Act provides a tax credit to defray the expenses of setting up and operating a new retirement plan. Costs paid or in-curred in tax years beginning after 2001 (for plans established after that date) are eligible for a non-refundable income tax credit equal to 50 percent of the first $1,000 in administrative and retirement-education expenses for each of the first three years of the plan.

The 50 percent of qualifying expenses that is off-set by the tax credit is not deductible; the other 50 percent (and all other expenses) is deductible as it is currently. The credit is available only to an employer that did not employ more than 100 employees who earned more than $5,000 in the preceding year. Also, at least one employee who is not highly compen-sated must be covered by the plan.

	2001 Tax Act	Current Law
Deductible start-up cost	$1,000	$1,000
Plan education expense	$1,000	$1,000
Total qualifying expenses	$2,000	$2,000
Credit	$500	$0
Total deductible expenses	$1,500	$2,000
Tax savings* including credit	$1,085	$780
Net cost of plan	$915	$1,220

* Assuming a 38.6% tax bracket for individual owner

Waiver of User Fees

The 2001 Tax Act relieves employer plans with 100 or fewer employees, and at least one participant who is not highly compensated, from paying a user fee for an IRS determination letter request regarding the plan's qualified status during its first five years (or the end of any remedial amendment period that begins within those first five years). This user fee waiver applies to determination letter requests made after December 31, 2001.

"Top-Heavy" Rules

So-called top-heavy retirement plans—those in which key employees receive more than 60 percent of the contributions or benefits—must provide certain minimum benefits or contribution levels to less-key employees and vest those benefits earlier than other plans are required to do. The 2001 Tax Act modifies the top-heavy rules effective for years beginning after 2001. A "key employee" is one who, during the prior year, was an officer with compensation in excess of $130,000, a 5 percent owner, or a 1 percent owner with compensation in excess of $150,000.

Also, only distributions made in the year prior to the determination date (and in-service distributions during the previous five years) are taken into account when deciding whether the plan is top-heavy. Matching contributions may be taken into account in satisfying the minimum benefit requirements. Another change is that a safe-harbor 401(k) plan is not a top-heavy plan, and matching or nonelective contributions provided under a safe-harbor plan may be taken into account in satisfying the minimum contribution requirements for top-heavy plans. Finally, the 2001 Tax Act provides that frozen defined benefit plans (or plans in which no key employee or former key employee benefits under the plan) are exempt from the minimum benefit requirements.

Increased Deduction Limits

The 2001 Tax Act made a variety of changes that can substantially raise an employer's maximum deductions for retirement plan contributions, effective for years beginning after 2001. These changes include:

- The deduction limit for stock bonus and profit sharing plans is increased from 15 percent of eligible compensation to 25 percent, and money purchase pension plans generally are to be treated like profit sharing or stock bonus plans for purposes of the deduction limits.

- Employee elective deferrals are no longer subject to deduction limits and will not be taken into account for purposes of applying the deduction limits to other types of contributions.
- For purposes of the deduction limits, the definition of "compensation" includes salary reduction amounts under a Section 125 cafeteria plan and 401(k) elective deferrals.

Observation: These changes will eliminate the need to have a profit sharing plan in tandem with a money purchase plan because they provide the maximum deduction of 25 percent of compensation. Tandem plans are currently the industry standard for small, closely held businesses, such as medical practices, that are attempting to accumulate and deduct maximum benefits for owner-employees. In addition to the advantages of administering only a single plan, the mandatory contribution required by the money purchase plan can be eliminated.

Observation: In addition to the increase in the deduction limit from 15 percent to 25 percent of compensation, the increase to $200,000 in the amount of compensation that may be used to figure allowable contributions and the increase to $40,000 in allowable annual additions will increase deductions for profit sharing plan contributions. These combined changes will allow owners of small, closely held businesses, especially those with few employees, to maximize their plan benefits without the complications of tandem plans. For 2002, for example, a company may deduct a full $40,000 contribution to a profit sharing plan made on behalf of a higher-paid employee (25 percent of up to $200,000 of compensation, but not more than the $40,000 limit on annual additions). For 2001, by comparison, the maximum deductible contribution in this situation is only $25,500 (15 percent of up to $170,000 of compensation).

Observation: An owner of a small, closely held business whose compensation is less than the $160,000 needed to obtain the maximum $40,000 deduction for 2001 can increase the contribution through the use of a 401(k) plan. The employee elective deferral to the 401(k) plan will not count toward the 25 percent of compensation deduction limit, even though it does count toward the $40,000 limit.

Estate Tax Changes

One of the most fundamental changes in the 2001 Tax Act is the gradual repeal of the federal estate tax. The estate tax—and another death tax called the generation-skipping transfer (GST) tax—begins to phase out starting in 2002, and will be eliminated entirely in 2010. The gift tax is not repealed, but its effect may be reduced under certain circumstances. As with the income tax provisions, all of the gift tax changes in the 2001 Tax Act are scheduled to sunset after 2010. Therefore, the repeal of the estate tax will last for only one year (2010) unless Congress makes further changes that are signed into law. Accompanying the repeal of the estate tax are some income tax changes that may cause appreciation in some of a decedent's property to be subject to income tax. Currently, all appreciation in property that occurred during a decedent's life escapes capital gains taxation. These and other changes will cause many people to reconsider and revise their estate plans.

Phase-Down of the Estate Tax
The gradual repeal of the estate tax begins in 2002 by:

• Increasing the amount that is shielded from estate tax.
• Reducing the top estate tax rate.

Exemption Increases. For 2001, the combined amount that anyone can give away during his or her lifetime or bequeath at death to anyone other than a spouse without paying gift or estate tax is $675,000.

There is no limit on the amount that can be given or left to a spouse. Under the 2001 Tax Act, this exempt amount increases to $1 million in 2002 for both estate and gift tax purposes. Thereafter, the exemption amount increases gradually to $3.5 million in 2009 for estate tax purposes, and remains at $1 million for gift tax purposes. (The GST exemption amount, which is $1,060,000 in 2001, will continue to be indexed for inflation in 2002 and 2003, and then will increase in tandem with the estate tax exemption amount until both taxes are repealed in 2010.) The gift tax will continue to apply to lifetime transfers totaling more than $1 million (not including up-to-$11,000 [in 2002] annual exclusion gifts) made to anyone, except a spouse.

 Observation: The 2001 Tax Act did not increase the $10,000 gift tax annual exclusion ($20,000 for most married couples), which allows relatively modest tax-free gifts to be made each year to an unlimited number of people. However, under existing law this amount can be raised in the future to reflect inflation and has been raised to $11,000 ($22,000 for couples) for 2002.

Caution: The increased estate tax exemption will require taxpayers to reexamine their estate plans if their wills and those of their spouses contain "bypass" or "credit-shelter" trusts, which many wills do in order to ensure that both spouses' estates receive the full estate tax exemption. These bequests are intended to leave the maximum amounts that can be passed on to children or other heirs (or in trusts for their benefits) without incurring estate tax. These provisions were designed around the exemption amounts ranging from the current $675,000 to $1 million (to which the exemption had been scheduled to be raised in 2006). As the exemption increases under the 2001 Tax Act, however, these arrangements will be funded with larger and larger amounts, and possibly all, of a decedent's assets, sometimes leaving nothing outright for the surviving spouse.

Rate Reduction. The 2001 Tax Act reduces the maximum estate and gift tax rates that apply to transfers above the exemption amount. The highest estate and gift tax rate—currently 55 percent—will fall to 50 percent in 2002, then gradually decline to 45 percent in 2009. Beginning in 2010, the top gift tax rate is scheduled to decline to 35 percent, which is the top individual tax rate provided under the 2001 Tax Act. The Act repeals the phase-out of the graduated rates (an extra 5 percent tax that applied to certain gifts or estates greater than $10 million) after 2001. The estate, GST, and gift tax rates and exemptions, from now through 2011, are represented in the following table.

Year-by-Year Transfer Tax Rates and Exemptions

Year	Estate Tax Exemption	GST Tax Exemption	Gift Tax Exemption	Highest Estate, GST, and Gift Tax Rates
2001	$675,000	$1,060,000	$675,000	55%
2002	$1 million	$1.1 million	$1 million	50%
2003	$1 million	$1.1 million (indexed)	$1 million	49%
2004	$1.5 million	$1.5 million	$1 million	48%
2005	$1.5 million	$1.5 million	$1 million	47%
2006	$2 million	$2 million	$1 million	46%
2007	$2 million	$2 million	$1 million	45%
2008	$2 million	$2 million	$1 million	45%
2009	$3.5 million	$3.5 million	$1 million	45%
2010	N/A (taxes repealed)	N/A (taxes repealed)	$1 million	35% (Gift tax), 0% (Estate and GST tax)
2011 and later	$1 million	$1,060,000 (indexed)	$1 million	55%

Loss of Credit for State Death Taxes

Existing law allows a credit against federal estate tax for state death taxes paid at a decedent's death. The credit can be approximately 16 percent of the estate. Every state imposes a state death tax at least equal to this credit to absorb the benefit of the credit against the estate tax. The 2001 Tax Act phases out the state death tax credit that is allowed against the federal estate tax. The credit will be 75 percent of the current credit for people who die in 2002, 50 percent in 2003, and 25 percent in 2004. In 2005, the state death tax credit will be repealed and replaced by a deduction for those taxes actually paid to any state.

Observation: The credit represents an important source of revenue for many states. It is anticipated that some will enact their own estate taxes to compensate for the repeal of this credit, a factor that should be considered when people decide where to live in retirement.

Loss of Full-Basis Step-Up

Repeal of the estate tax in 2010 will be accompanied by the repeal of the present rules, which provide that a beneficiary's basis (the cost used to figure the gain when property is sold or otherwise disposed of) in assets, acquired from a decedent, is generally "stepped-up" to fair market value as of the date of death. This basis step-up eliminates capital gains tax liability on appreciation in inherited assets that occurred during the decedent's lifetime. Those who inherit property from decedents who die in 2010, however, will receive only a limited basis step-up, which will eliminate income tax on a maximum of $1.3 million of gain that accrued during the decedent's life. Property inherited by a surviving spouse will get an additional $3 million of basis increase, thereby allowing a total basis increase of up to $4.3 million for property transferred to a surviving spouse. (If the decedent was a nonresident alien, the aggregate basis increase would be limited to $60,000, regardless of the beneficiary's relationship to the decedent.)

In addition to the allowable basis step-up, an estate or its beneficiaries who acquire the principal residence of a decedent who dies in 2010 will be able to qualify for tax-free treatment on its sale if that decedent could have qualified. The result can be an additional income tax-free gain of a maximum of $250,000.

The estate's executor will choose which of the decedent's assets will receive the basis increase. (There will be a number of restrictions on basis allocation to avoid the creation of artificial tax losses and other effects not intended by the rule.) Certain additional basis increases will be permitted so that the decedent's losses that were not deducted are not wasted. After permitted basis increases have been exhausted, beneficiaries will receive a basis in the property equal to the decedent's adjusted basis (referred to as a carryover basis) or the fair market value of the property on the date of the decedent's death, whichever is less. For property owned jointly by spouses, only the decedent's half of the property will be eligible for a basis increase.

Donors and estate executors will be required to report information about certain transfers to the IRS and to donees and estate beneficiaries, including basis and holding period information.

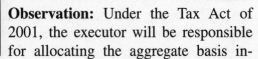 **Observation:** Under the Tax Act of 2001, the executor will be responsible for allocating the aggregate basis increase limits among different assets and various beneficiaries of the property. If some beneficiaries receive higher-basis property, the other beneficiaries may be burdened with higher capital gains if they sell the inherited property.

Estate planning may help minimize the potential for family strife or litigation over basis allocation issues after a benefactor's death.

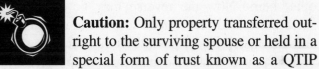 **Caution:** Only property transferred outright to the surviving spouse or held in a special form of trust known as a QTIP (qualified terminable interest property) trust qualifies for the additional $3 million of basis increase for property passing to surviving spouses. Many persons now have testamentary plans in which bequests to surviving spouses are held in other forms of trusts that qualify for the marital deduction for estate tax purposes, but won't qualify for the $3 million basis increase.

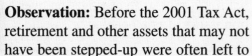

Observation: For those interested in charitable giving, retirement assets are an excellent choice of assets to leave to charity. Because retirement assets qualify for a step-up in basis neither before nor after the repeal of the estate tax and, generally, don't even qualify for capital gains rates, income tax consequences can be minimized by leaving the retirement assets to charity.

Observation: Before the 2001 Tax Act, retirement and other assets that may not have been stepped-up were often left to the surviving spouse rather than to children or other heirs. Now the reverse may be desirable, since there could be a need to use the maximum amount of step-up for post-2010 transfers to a surviving spouse. But this decision is complicated by other considerations: That only a surviving spouse may make certain favorable IRA withdrawal elections is one example. Careful planning is required.

More Conservation Easements Deductible

The 2001 Tax Act expands the availability of special estate tax treatment for qualified conservation easements by eliminating the requirement that the land be located within a certain distance of a metropolitan area, national park, wilderness area, or an Urban National Forest as designated by the USDA

Forest Service. A qualified conservation easement may now be claimed for estate tax purposes with respect to any land that is located in the United States or its possessions. These provisions are effective for estates of decedents who die after 2000.

 Observation: This liberalization may lead to increased use of this technique, which may be attractive to environmentally minded landowners.

Qualified Domestic Trusts

A qualified domestic trust (QDOT) is a special trust that qualifies for the estate tax marital deduction when the surviving spouse is not a U.S. citizen. Generally, the estate tax is deferred until the death of the surviving spouse, at which time an estate tax based upon the value of the trust principal that remains must be paid. If distributions of trust principal are paid out to the surviving spouse before death, estate tax also would be payable based on the value of those distributions. Under the 2001 Tax Act, the QDOT principal would escape estate taxation if the surviving spouse dies in 2010. However, any distribution of principal from a QDOT to a living spouse will remain subject to the estate tax through 2020, but would be free of estate tax in 2021. But because 2021 will occur after the December 31, 2010, sunset date, this provision is, in effect, voided by the Act.

Observation: It is possible to avoid estate tax entirely in the case of QDOTs that are established before 2010. QDOTs, therefore, should be considered when planning the estate of anyone married to a non–U.S. citizen.

Installment Payment of Estate Taxes

The 2001 Tax Act expands availability of estate tax installment payment provisions for estates of business owners. To alleviate the liquidity problems of estates comprised significantly of closely held business interests, qualifying estates may defer the estate tax attributable to the closely held business on an installment basis for up to 14 years at a low interest rate. The 2001 Tax Act expands availability of installment payment relief to certain qualified lending and finance business interests, as well as to certain holding company stock. In addition, the new law increases from 15 to 45 the cap on the number of partners that can be included in a partnership or shareholders in a closely held corporation and still be eligible for installment payment relief. These changes are effective for decedents dying after 2001.

To qualify for the installment payment relief, a lending and finance business must meet several technical requirements. In particular, its stock or debt could not have been publicly traded at any time within the three years immediately preceding the decedent's death. Also, an estate relying on the relief for qualified lending or finance businesses under the new law must make the installment payments in five years rather than 14. Similarly, an estate taking advantage of the new holding company rules must pay the tax over nine years.

 Observation: This provision provides additional relief for an often overlooked issue of estate planning: ensuring sufficient liquidity to pay estate taxes. By liberalizing the rules, additional businesses can qualify for this relief. However, they must still comprise a certain percentage of the total estate assets; other requirements apply as well.

Repeal of Estate Tax Break for Family Businesses

The 2001 Tax Act repeals the special estate tax deduction for qualified family-owned business interests (QFOBI) beginning in 2004.

 Observation: This deduction was repealed because the increase in the regular estate tax exemption (discussed above) to $1.5 million in 2004 will exceed the total amount of the qualified family-owned business interest deduction, which is limited to $1.3 million, less the estate tax exemption amount. Thus, estates of family-owned business owners will not be hurt by the repeal, but will not be entitled to an estate tax exemption any greater than other estates.

Estate Tax Recovery Opportunity for Some Farm Families

Estates of farmers and certain other business owners may qualify for estate tax breaks by valuing the decedent's business realty at its special-use value, for example, as farmland, rather than at the land's value at its highest and best use, say, as a residential subdivision. Generally, to qualify for this break, the decedent's family members must continue to use the property for its specially valued purpose. Cash rentals of the property may cause recapture of the special-use valuation estate tax break and, at one time, that was the case even for cashlease arrangements with the decedent's spouse or lineal descendants.

The 2001 Tax Act waives the statute of limitations for a refund claim or credit on estate taxes paid on certain specially valued farm property if the tax overpayment resulted from applying certain net-cash lease arrangements with spouses and lineal descendants of the decedent that may have been considered a nonqualified use of the property. These claims are now permitted, even though they otherwise would be barred by the statute of limitations, provided that the claim is made within one year of June 7, 2001.

What's Next

In this chapter, we have explained the far-reaching effects of the Tax Act of 2001, shown the importance of planning to adjust for its continuing changes, and reviewed the law's main provisions. Now it is time to discuss in detail how taxpayers should handle their investments to take advantage of the law.

It is only fair that when people profit from investments, they must hand over some of their gains to the IRS. But no one has any obligation to pay any more than is legally due, and it is as wise as it is legitimate to plan an investment strategy to take maximum advantage of what is provided in the tax law. In the next chapter, we will explain how the new law changes the playing field for investors.

YEAR-ROUND
TAX PLANNING
STRATEGIES

Investments and Stock Options

No investor—whether in stocks, bonds, sophisticated hedge funds, or simple certificates of deposit—can afford to ignore the effects that the 2001 tax law will have on managing a portfolio. The law's continuing changes over the next decade are likely to require continuous adjustments in order to minimize one's federal tax bill.

To the extent that it reduces regular income tax rates, the law reduces tax liability for interest, dividends, and short-term capital gains. Thus, even though the tax law does not directly affect long-term gains on assets held for more than a year, its effect is to reduce the marginal advantage of long-term gains, making them relatively less attractive. But their advantages are still strong, particularly since earlier tax changes that became effective in 2001 have added to the tax benefits of gains on assets held for more than five years.

Investors must also consider the effect of the Alternative Minimum Tax (AMT) on their market gains. The benefit of municipal bond interest, for instance, is lessened for investors who are subject to the AMT. The new law does provide modest relief from the AMT for the years 2001 through 2004, but after that the tax reverts to its terms before the cut—a fact that investors should keep in mind in planning for 2005.

Many taxpayers will choose to convert some of their investments to newly liberalized Coverdell Education Savings Accounts or college tuition savings plans for their children. We describe these strategies in depth in Chapter 5 of this book.

Investors should also take note that the phasing out of the estate tax has a catch-22 clause: In 2010, securities in an estate will no longer escape all capital gains when passed on to an heir. Under the new law, the heirs' tax-free gains on inherited property will be limited to a total of $1.3 million. An additional $3 million of gains on property received by a surviving spouse will also be able to escape capital gains tax. Until now, many investors have taken it as nearly axiomatic that securities with very large gains should be reserved for their heirs. In some instances, that strategy may have to be rethought because the 2001 Tax Act places a limit on gains that can pass to heirs tax-free in 2010.

In this chapter, we will discuss in detail the many ways taxpayers can adjust their investment options to minimize the taxes they pay under the new law. We include a checklist of ideas to consider as readers plan their investment strategies for the decade to come.

Capital Gains

Capital gains income results when you sell or exchange a capital asset. Examples of capital assets include the shares of stock or securities you own, your personal residence, or a work of art.

Favorable Rates

Long-term capital gains (gains from capital assets held for more than one year) are usually taxed at a maximum rate of 20 percent when you sell the property.

Example: An individual in the top tax bracket (39.1 percent in 2001) sells stock that he purchased over a year ago, recognizing a gain of $10,000. His long-term capital gains tax is $2,000—20 percent of $10,000. Had he sold the stock before owning it for more than a year for the same $10,000 gain, his tax liability would be $3,910—39.1 percent of $10,000.

Observation: The lower tax rates on long-term capital gains make stock investments more advantageous and reduce the attractiveness of "ordinary income" investments, such as regular IRAs (but not Roth IRAs), tax deferred annuities, and fixed income investments. However, the 2001 Tax Act's income tax rate cuts (see Chapter 1) will diminish this advantage somewhat.

Observation: The capital gains rate is increased effectively in some tax brackets by the itemized deduction cutback and the personal exemption phase-out (see Chapter 8). Loss of personal exemptions and itemized deductions will be less of a problem in the future, because the 2001 Tax Act gradually eliminates these hidden tax rate boosters beginning in 2006. Until then, the marginal tax rate on net long-term capital gains for higher-income individuals may be 22 percent or higher, depending on personal circumstances.

Exceptions to the 20 Percent Rate

Take note that the long-term capital gains rate is only 10 percent on gain that would be taxed at no more than 15 percent were it ordinary income.

Example: Assume your regular income (wages, interest, and dividends) is taxed at no more than 15 percent, and you sell stock that you purchased over a year ago for a gain of $10,000, all of which would be taxed to you at no more than 15 percent if it were ordinary income. You will be subject to long-term capital gains tax of $1,000 (10 percent of $10,000), not $2,000 (20 percent of $10,000).

A higher maximum tax rate of 28 percent applies to long-term capital gains from the sale of collectibles (such as art or antiques), and to one-half of the long-term capital gains from the sale of qualified small-business stock (the other half of the gain on the sale of such stock, up to certain limits, is tax-free).

Example: An individual who is not an antiques dealer sells an oil painting from his personal collection, which he has owned for many years, for $10,000 more than he paid for it. His capital gains tax liability is $2,800—28 percent of $10,000.

Even Better Rates for Five-Year Gains

There has always been a required minimum holding period to qualify for long-term capital gains rates. Over the years it has varied from more than six months to more than two years. But starting in 2001, capital gains rates that are even lower than the standard ones—18 percent and 8 percent—will apply to certain five-year gains on capital assets.

• *18 percent rate.* This rate, instead of the usual 20 percent rate, will apply to capital gains from property held for more than five years if the holding period for the property begins in 2001 or later.

• *8 percent rate.* This rate, instead of the 10 percent rate, will apply to capital gains from property held for more than five years and sold in 2001 or later. There is no requirement for the holding period to have begun after 2000 to qualify for this low rate, as there is to qualify for the 18 percent rate.

 **Observation:** The availability of the 8 percent rate for those in the lowest tax bracket presents a great family-income-splitting opportunity. You can transfer stock or other assets that you have held for many years to your low-bracket children or grandchildren, who can then sell the assets (after they turn 14, to avoid the kiddie tax) and qualify for the 8 percent rate to the extent the gains don't push their income above the 15 percent bracket (about $27,000 for singles and $45,000 for married couples in 2001; about $28,000 and $46,700, respectively, for 2002). This is possible because your holding period carries over to recipients of the property when you make the gift. As a result, what would have been your 20 percent capital gains tax liability becomes your children's or grandchildren's 8 percent capital gains tax—a 12-percentage-point tax savings.

Example: An individual in the top tax bracket (39.1 percent in 2001) owns stock purchased more than five years ago on which he has a $10,000 gain. If he sold the stock in 2001 to help pay his grandson's college tuition, for example, his long-term capital gains tax liability would be $2,000—20 percent of $10,000. If he gives the stock to his 17-year-old grandson, who has only a few thousand dollars of taxable income this year from a summer job, the tax bill would be cut to $800 on his grandson's sale of the stock, saving $1,200.

 Caution: Gain on a post-2000 gift of property that was purchased before 2001, however, will not qualify for the 18 percent rate, because the holding period for the person receiving the property is considered to have begun when the stock was originally bought. Since that was before 2001, gain on any later sale by a person in a tax bracket above 15 percent will be taxed at the 20 percent rate, even if he or she actually held the asset for more than five years before the sale.

 Caution: Gain on stock received from the post-2000 exercise of a stock option granted before 2001 will also not qualify for the 18 percent rate. That's because for the purposes of qualifying for the 18 percent rate, the holding period for the option stock is considered to begin on the date of the option grant.

Qualifying Current Holdings for 18 Percent Rate

You can qualify property purchased before 2001 for the 18 percent rate by electing to treat it as having been sold and repurchased at the beginning of 2001. Readily tradable stock will be deemed to have been sold and repurchased at its closing price on the first business day after January 1, 2001. The deemed sale and repurchase of other capital assets, such as real estate or artwork, is treated as made at their fair market value on January 1, 2001. Making this election will start a new post-2000 holding period without requiring you to actually go through the trouble and expense of selling and repurchasing the property. But keep in mind that making the election will also trigger capital gains taxation for 2001. So you will have to pay tax now on your paper gains in order to get a slightly reduced rate five or more years in the future.

Observation: Making the deemed-sale election for an asset will generally be wise only when the current gain is small, future gains are expected to be large, and it is almost certain that the property will be held for another five years. Otherwise, the loss of earnings on the funds used to pay the accelerated capital gains tax could easily be more than the potential savings from the reduced rate on a future sale.

Observation: If you make the deemed-sale election, you are, in effect, betting that Congress won't reduce future capital gains rates—a change for which there is some support, especially in the House of Representatives.

 Observation: You don't have to decide whether to make a deemed-sale election for particular property until you file your 2001 return. (In fact, you have until October 15, 2002, to make the election on an amended or extended return.) If you have capital losses in 2001, you can use them to offset gain from the deemed-sale election so that you won't have additional taxes due for capital gains resulting from the election.

 Caution: Keep in mind that once you make a deemed-sale election you cannot revoke it.

 Caution: You should not make a deemed-sale election for property on which you have a loss because the loss will not be allowed. That is, it cannot be used to offset capital gains on your current tax return or in the future. In other words, the election can't be used as a way to generate losses that offset other capital gains.

Netting Rules

Favorable capital gains rates and the long-term capital gains holding requirements may influence when you sell property, which in turn affects your tax bill. When calculating your capital gains income, keep in mind that the following ordering rules apply to netting capital gains and losses. The rules are fairly complicated, but they should generally produce the lowest overall tax. Long-term capital gains and losses (for this purpose, "long-term" refers to a holding period of more than one year) are divided into three groups determined by tax rates:

- a 28 percent group (for long-term capital gains from the sale of collectibles such as art or antiques, and half of the long-term capital gains from the sale of qualified small-business stock);
- a 25 percent group (for part of the gain from the sale of depreciable real estate); and
- a 20 percent group (for long-term capital gains from the sale of all other capital assets).

Netting of long-term gains and losses occurs freely within a tax rate group.

Net losses within a long-term tax rate group are used to offset net gains from the long-term tax rate group with the highest tax rate. If there are net losses remaining, they offset gains from the next-highest tax rate group.

Example: Assume that there will be net losses in the 20 percent tax rate group. The net losses first offset any net gains in the 28 percent tax rate group, then offset net gains in the 25 percent tax rate group.

Long-term capital loss carryovers from 2000 offset net gains for the highest long-term tax rate group first, then the other long-term tax rate groups in descending order.

Example: A net long-term capital loss carryover from 2000 first offsets net 28 percent capital gains, then net 25 percent capital gains, and finally net 20 percent capital gains.

Net short-term capital losses offset net long-term capital gains beginning with the highest tax rate group.

Example: A net short-term capital loss first offsets net 28 percent capital gains, then net 25 percent capital gains, and finally net 20 percent capital gains.

Net long-term capital losses can offset short-term capital gains.

Observation: On your 2001 and later returns, this netting process will also separate out any gains and losses from sales of five-year property that is eligible for even lower rates, as explained above.

Capital Losses

Capital losses are deductible dollar for dollar against capital gains. In addition, you may deduct up to $3,000 in net capital losses (either short-term or long-term) each year against your ordinary income (such as wages). Amounts in excess of this figure may be carried forward indefinitely.

Wash Sale Rule

If you hold securities or mutual funds that have substantially declined in value and you do not think they will recover anytime soon, you might want to sell them to realize the loss now. If you want to maintain a position in this investment category, you can repurchase other assets of similar quality. But you should not immediately repurchase "substantially identical" (the IRS uses this term to broaden the prohibited repurchase to securities and mutual funds that are not identical to what you had sold but are of the same category and type) assets because the "wash sale" rule will prevent you from taking a tax loss this year unless you wait at least 31 days after the sale before repurchasing any "substantially identical" assets. If you trigger the wash sale rule, your loss will be suspended and added to your cost basis (the amount you pay for the security plus other acquisition costs, such as brokerage commissions; this amount is then used to figure your gain or loss when you sell the security) in the replacement securities, which will reduce your taxable gain or increase your loss when the replacement securities are sold.

To avoid the wash sale rule, you must buy the "substantially identical" assets at least 31 days before or after the sale of the securities or mutual funds. The disadvantage of this is that in the first case you risk doubling your losses if the value of the investment continues to fall while you are doubled up in it, and in the second case you risk loss of potential price increases if you are out of the investment for 31 or more days.

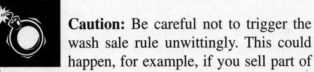

Caution: Be careful not to trigger the wash sale rule unwittingly. This could happen, for example, if you sell part of your investment in a security or fund at a loss, and a dividend paid on the remaining shares is automatically reinvested in the same shares within the restricted 30-day period.

Observation: It is always helpful to review your realized and unrealized capital gains and losses, as well as loss carryovers. This is especially important if you want to reduce your tax bills in future years. If you have unrealized capital losses, consider taking them to the extent of realized capital gains. Also, you may wish to realize another $3,000 in losses this year to offset that amount of otherwise taxable ordinary income. If you have already realized net capital losses over $3,000 this year, you may decide to move up the realization of capital gains by making the deemed-sale election explained on page 80, since this could reduce your future tax on the gains by 2 percent. There is no other tax benefit to moving up the recognition of gains to offset losses that have been recognized on this year's return. Keep in mind that you must first offset long-term losses against long-term gains and short-term losses against short-term gains before netting the remaining long- and short-term gains or losses against each other.

Protecting and Postponing Stock Gains

You can no longer effectively use the "short sale against the box" technique to safely lock in your gains while postponing realizing capital gains from the sale of appreciated assets until the following year, as you could in the past. Two other strategies remain:

• *Buying put options covering stock you own.* (A put option is an options contract that entitles the holder to sell a number of shares [usually 100] of the underlying common stock at a stated price on or before a fixed expiration date.) Under this strategy, any decline in the price of the stock is likely to be offset, at least in part, by an increase in the price of the put option.

• *Writing covered call options.* (A covered call is a trade that involves buying the underlying stock and selling a call against the stock position.) This means that you write (sell) call options against the stock you own. If the stock price drops, some of your unrealized gain will be lost, but the loss will be offset, at least in part, by a profit resulting from the premium received from the sale of the option.

More complex strategies include collars and variable prepaid forwards. Capital gains can also be deferred or possibly eliminated through the use of charitable remainder trusts.

Passive Activity Losses

Investment losses are limited by a complex set of provisions known as the passive activity loss rules. In general, losses and credits from passive activities can offset only passive income and may not be used against earned income (such as salaries) or portfolio income (such as dividends or interest). Passive activities generally include any business or investment activity in which you do not materially participate.

Rental activities (for example, where you own a vacation home and rent it out to others) are treated as passive, with certain exceptions.

 Observation: Real estate professionals may deduct losses and credits from rental real estate activities in which they materially participate.

Consider the following year-end strategies if you have unusable passive losses:

• Purchase investments that generate passive income.
• Become a material participant in the activity, if feasible, by increasing your level of involvement.
• Sell or dispose of your entire interest in the passive activity to free up the losses.

 Observation: Even more restrictive rules apply to certain types of passive activities, such as "publicly traded partnerships." Publicly traded partnership losses can offset only publicly traded partnership income, not income from other types of passive activities.

Careful Record Keeping:
Identification of Securities

If you hold many securities, knowing when and at what price you purchased them will help you maximize your tax savings when you sell them. Because of differences in holding periods and bases, a sale may mean either short-term or long-term gain or loss, depending on which securities you sell or are deemed to have sold. Accurate record keeping is therefore critical to minimizing taxes. If you redeem an actual security certificate at the time of sale, the securities sold will be those identified on the certificate. If one certificate represents securities acquired on different dates or at different prices, you can tell the broker (in writing) which lot you are selling. If you do not identify securities, you will generally be deemed to have sold the first securities acquired, which would have the longest holding period (and therefore might be taxed at a lower rate), but may also have the largest taxable gain.

Observation: Mutual fund shares are usually treated in the same way as other securities, or you can use their average cost when determining basis. Once you apply the earliest-cost or average-cost method to a mutual fund, you must continue to use that method in future years for that mutual fund.

Observation: When selling stock that has risen in value, you can lower your taxes by identifying the securities in which you have the highest bases as the ones that are being sold. However, if you hold these securities for one year or less, any gain will be short-term, subject to tax at ordinary income rates.

Tax-Exempt and Taxable Bonds

It generally makes sense to invest in tax-exempt securities only if you are in a high federal income tax bracket and live in a high income tax state. However, depending upon the date on which the bond matures and current market conditions, some long-term municipal bonds may produce a higher after-tax yield even in the 15 percent bracket (see Chapter 8). The decision also hinges on the size of the interest rate differential between taxable and tax-free bonds.

When deciding whether to invest in tax-exempt or taxable bonds, choose the type that will give you the highest after-tax yield within your risk tolerance limits, taking into account the bonds' credit quality and liquidity. As you calculate the after-tax yield on a taxable bond, remember to include your state tax rate. If you invest in tax-exempt investments issued by a political subdivision in a state other than your state of residence, the income is usually taxable on your resident state return, even though it is free from federal tax.

Taxable "Tax-Exempt" Bonds

Certain tax-exempt bonds ("private activity bonds") are tax-exempt for regular income tax purposes but are taxable for the AMT. Private activity bonds have a slightly higher yield than bonds that are exempt from both regular tax and AMT.

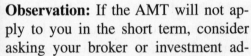 **Observation:** If the AMT will not apply to you in the short term, consider asking your broker or investment adviser to offer you the higher-yielding private activity bonds.

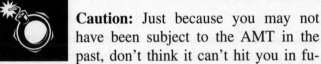 **Caution:** Just because you may not have been subject to the AMT in the past, don't think it can't hit you in future years. Unlike regular income tax rates, AMT rate brackets and exemption amounts are not indexed annually for inflation. So AMT liability has been creeping down the income line and has begun to hit many who are squarely in the middle class. The 2001 Tax Act provided modest AMT relief beginning in 2001—but only through 2004 (see Chapter 1 for details). So carefully consider your future AMT exposure before purchasing the higher-yielding private activity bonds.

Bond Premium or Discount

If you pay more than face value for a bond, you have paid a premium for it. This is usually the case if the bond's coupon rate is higher than the prevailing rate for newly issued comparable bonds at the time of purchase. You must amortize the premium of a tax-exempt bond by reducing its basis, but you have a choice whether or not to amortize the premium of a taxable bond by offsetting it against the bond's interest. If you elect to amortize the bond premium, you must do so for all bonds you own or later acquire. If you don't amortize the bond premium, you will usually have a capital loss when you sell or redeem the bond.

If you purchase a bond at a discount from its original issuer, the difference between the issue price and the redemption price (called "original issue discount," or OID) is interest income. In almost all cases, a portion of this interest must be included in income each year even though it isn't received until the bond is redeemed. Taxable OID bonds, therefore, are best suited for individuals if they are held in tax deferred accounts, such as IRA or 401(k) accounts, or tax-exempt accounts, such as Roth IRAs.

The original issue discount rules don't apply to U.S. savings bonds, notes that mature in one year or less, or tax-exempt bonds (unless they have been stripped of their coupons).

If you buy a bond with a market discount—that is, a bond that has lost value since its issue date (usually because interest rates have risen since it was issued)—gain on its sale will in most cases be taxed as interest income to the extent of the accrued market discount. This also applies to municipals.

Florida Intangibles Trust

If you are a Florida resident and pay a significant amount of Florida intangibles tax each year, consider establishing a Florida Intangibles Trust or other vehicle that may exempt from the tax the value of your intangible assets (for example, stocks and bonds). Note that the impact of the Florida intangibles tax has been reduced significantly in the past couple of years, from 0.2 percent to 0.15 percent for 2000, and to 0.1 percent beginning in 2001.

 Observation: Include the cost of establishing and operating the Florida Intangible Trust or other vehicle when determining whether this planning idea makes sense for you.

Nonqualified Stock Options

Nonqualified stock options generate compensation income when they are exercised equal to the difference between the fair market value of the stock and the exercise price. Subsequent appreciation in the value of the option stock is taxed at favorable capital gains rates. Most individuals benefit by exercising these options shortly before the options expire, unless it is expected that the value of the options will be lost owing to a stock-value decline or other reason. Early exercise at or near the strike price gives up all the downside protection of the option. By holding off on exercise, you can benefit from the presumably increased stock value without making a cash investment in the stock. However, if the appreciation potential of the stock is expected to be great, early exercise can be advantageous because it minimizes the portion of the gain that will be taxed as compensation (at ordinary income rates) and maximizes the amount that will qualify for capital gains rates. The decision about when to exercise options should also take into account the amount of appreciation to date, the future prospects of the company, and, most important, the percent of net worth represented by company stock. Some option plans permit you to pay the exercise price in the form of existing shares, which can be helpful when cash is in short supply.

Withholding of federal income tax, Social Security, Medicare, and state and local taxes are all due when the options are exercised. If the stock option is exercised and then sold quickly, the cash generated from the sale can be used to help satisfy these withholding obligations. The gain generated may create a substantial tax liability, so additional planning may be necessary to come up with the cash needed to pay taxes due April 15.

Observation: If all the stock is going to be held after you have exercised your option, it is important to plan how to satisfy these withholding obligations. Some plans allow the use of shares to cover withholding taxes. Some employers grant "phantom" stock in connection with nonqualified options, which can help cover withholding taxes.

Incentive Stock Options

The favorable long-term capital gains tax rates make incentive stock options particularly attractive. However, careful planning is needed to maximize the benefits of these options if the AMT is a concern.

For regular tax purposes, an incentive stock option (ISO) exercise is not a taxable event (state and local tax treatment may differ). However, at exercise the difference between the fair market value of the stock on the date of the exercise and the exercise price is an add-back to an individual's alternative minimum taxable income.

ISOs are subject to a number of requirements imposed by the Tax Code that do not apply to nonqualified compensatory stock options. For example:

• ISOs can't be issued at a strike price lower than the value of the option stock on the date the options are granted.

- ISOs can't be exercised more than 10 years after the options are granted.
- ISOs aren't transferable except at death, and during the grantee's lifetime may be exercised only by the grantee.
- ISOs must be exercised within 90 days of termination of employment to be treated as ISOs.
- There is a $100,000 annual limit on ISO grants.
- To get favorable ISO tax treatment, the ISO stock can't be sold within a year of option exercise or within two years of the option grant. If option stock is sold before either of these two periods has run, the option is treated as a nonqualified option, usually resulting in compensation income to the option holder.

Observation: For those not otherwise subject to the AMT, ISO exercises should be timed to occur over the life of the option (usually 10 years) to minimize the AMT impact and to start the more than one year holding period needed to qualify for the 20 percent capital gains tax rate. If little or no planning goes into an ISO exercise, you could be required to pay taxes earlier or in larger amounts than may be necessary.

Caution: Care should also be taken not to sell or otherwise dispose of the stock received from an ISO exercise before one year from the exercise date or two years from the grant date, whichever is later, because before that time you will be taxed at ordinary income rates.

Observation: Stock received on a post-2000 exercise of options that were issued before 2001 won't qualify for the reduced 18 percent capital gains rate even if the stock is held for more than five years. That's because the holding period of the stock for 18 percent tax treatment is considered as beginning on the date the option was granted to you—and in order to qualify for the 18 percent rate, the holding period needs to begin in 2001 or later.

Observation: It is best to exercise ISOs early in the year if the AMT is likely to be paid. This gives you the flexibility to sell before year-end and avoid the AMT if the stock tanks. In this case you will only pay ordinary income tax on the actual gain, rather than the AMT on the spread between the fair market value at exercise and the exercise price.

Idea Checklist

☐ Carefully consider whether your portfolio should be weighted more heavily in equities, eligible for capital gains tax rates, and less heavily in assets that produce ordinary income.

☐ Consider whether to make a deemed-sale election on your 2001 income tax return to qualify for even lower capital gains rates on capital assets you expect to hold for more than five years, especially if capital losses can offset the gain from the deemed sale.

☐ Make gifts of capital assets held for more than five years to your low-bracket children or grandchildren so the gains can be taxed at only 8 percent.

☐ Review your capital gains and capital loss positions before year-end. Try to offset capital gains with capital losses. Keep in mind the 30-day wash sale rule.

☐ Make full use of $3,000 in capital losses that can be used to offset your ordinary income.

☐ Determine whether tax-exempt bonds are an appropriate investment. If so, consider whether investing in "taxable" tax-exempts will improve your cash yield.

☐ Florida residents should consider ways to reduce their Florida intangibles tax liability.

☐ Executives with incentive stock options should exercise some of them if the AMT does not apply and hold the shares for more than one year (and two years from option grant) to ensure a maximum 20 percent capital gains rate.

This analysis of how the new tax law will affect investments is not intended as a magic formula that will instantly adjust portfolios to minimize taxes. Investors must chart their individual courses, depending on their goals, tolerance for risk, and specific circumstances. This chapter contains the necessary tools to begin that task.

A key goal for most taxpayers' investment strategies is, of course, to accumulate funds for retirement. The next chapter will assess the many ways in which the tax law of 2001 affects retirement savings—and finds that, on balance, taxpayers should be applauding the changes.

Retirement Planning

Thanks to the new tax law, most Americans are about to find that life after work can be more rewarding from a financial perspective and also potentially more secure than it was for their parents. The new law, however, also makes retirement planning more complicated. Congress has created major new incentives for retirement savings with more tax breaks than ever before. And the benefits will keep increasing for years to come.

This news is particularly welcome because retirement planning is more important now than ever. With employer-paid pensions becoming more rare every year and more businesses downsizing, wage earners face the prospect of financing more of their retirements with their own resources. For most people, retirement income is likely to come from three sources:

- Tax-favored retirement plans, perhaps including defined benefit pension plans, but more likely profit sharing, stock bonus, IRA and Roth IRA, and employer-sponsored savings plans. These include 401(k), 403(b) (for employees of tax-exempt organizations), SEP (simplified employee pension) and Keogh plans (for the self-employed), SIMPLE (savings incentive match plan for employees) plans for workers in firms with fewer than 100 employees, and 457 plans for government employees.
- A taxpayer's investments outside of tax-favored retirement plans.
- Social Security.

Under the new law, taxpayers will be allowed to increase their contributions to qualified savings plans, with workers age 50 and over permitted to make even more generous catch-up contributions—reaching, in some cases, as much as $5,000 a year by 2006. Also under the new law, high-income employees who don't qualify for Roth IRAs will be able to enroll in an employer-sponsored Roth incentive savings plan, to which they contribute after-tax funds but are allowed to withdraw the money and its gains tax-free with no fixed schedule. (Roth funds can even be left to an heir income tax-free.) Employer-matching contributions will be vested more rapidly, and the retirement plans will be more portable, allowing workers to transfer the funds when they change jobs. Low-income workers will get a tax credit for as much as 50 percent of the money they contribute to qualified retirement plans and IRAs that will reduce their taxes for the year of the contribution.

As always, taxpayers must keep in mind the benefits of capital gains tax breaks when planning for retirement. Retirement plans allow tax-free compounding of profits, but in most plans, pay-outs are taxed at ordinary income tax rates in the year they are received. Those who expect relatively high income in retirement should weigh the merits of forgoing the tax deferral, investing after-tax funds for retirement, and being taxed on sale at lower capital gains rates. (However, they should not forget that the Alternative Minimum Tax [AMT] could void much of the advantage.)

This chapter will detail valuable planning techniques and offer suggestions that can help to reduce overall tax bills and maximize income during retirement.

Employer Plans

Qualified Retirement Plans

When possible, you should think about participating in a qualified employer pension or profit sharing plan, 401(k) plan, 403(b) plan, Keogh, or simplified employee pension (SEP) plan. Qualified plans must meet complex participation, coverage, and non-discrimination requirements, allowing sponsoring employers to immediately deduct their contributions. Employer contributions on your behalf are not taxed to you until you receive them. Your contributions to these plans reduce your adjusted gross income (AGI) (within specified limits) and your current tax bill. This tax deferral is often achieved in exchange for reduced liquidity because you give up immediate access to the funds. However, some plans permit you to borrow up to allowable limits from your account, which gives you access to some of your savings if necessary. For plan years beginning after 2001, even owner-employees, such as sole proprietors, partners, and S corporation shareholders, will be able to borrow from their retirement plans just like other employees without getting hit with the prohibitive excise tax that previously applied.

 Observation: The savings incentive match plan for employees (SIMPLE) is available to employees of companies with 100 or fewer employees that do not have other types of retirement plans. Under this type of plan, employees may defer up to $6,500 for 2001. Employers that offer a SIMPLE generally must make a nonelective or matching contribution on behalf of each plan participant.

Observation: There is no longer a "combined plan limit," which in the past put a cap on contributions for highly compensated employees who participate in both an employer's pension plan and a profit sharing plan. Now, even if you are highly compensated, you can accumulate larger qualified retirement plan benefits.

There are two basic kinds of qualified employer retirement plans:

• defined contribution plans
• defined benefit plans

Defined Contribution Plans

A defined contribution plan allows your company or you—or your company *and* you—to contribute a set amount each year to the plan. Contributions are set aside in an account for you and are invested on your behalf. Sometimes you have the right to determine how the contributions are invested. With a defined contribution plan, you are not guaranteed a set amount of benefits when you retire. Instead, you receive the amount in the account, which depends on how much was contributed to it and how successfully the funds were invested over the years. You get a statement at least once a year advising you of your current account balance.

Defined contribution plan benefits are portable, so if you change jobs, you can transfer your vested benefits to an IRA or possibly to your new employer's plan. Most defined benefit pension plans, on the contrary, don't make your vested benefit available before you reach retirement age, unless your benefit is very small (in which case the plan may cash you out).

The most common defined contribution plans are profit sharing plans, 401(k) plans, stock bonus plans, and employee stock ownership plans.

Bigger Contributions Allowed

The 2001 Tax Act increased the overall limit on amounts that may be added each year by you and your employer to defined contribution plans, including 401(k) plans and profit sharing plans, beginning with the 2002 plan year. The 2001 limit (the lesser of $35,000 or 25 percent of compensation) will be raised to the lesser of 100 percent of compensation or $40,000 (an amount that will be indexed for future inflation). The Tax Act also increased the amount of compensation that can be taken into account for retirement plan purposes from $170,000 to $200,000 beginning in 2002. This means that larger contributions and benefits are possible for the more highly compensated.

Caution: Highly paid employees may still not be allowed to take full advantage of the increased contribution limits after nondiscrimination tests are applied.

 Observation: While the 100 percent limit permits allocation to an individual account of the entire salary, the 25 percent limitation on deductions for all contributions will apply to prevent a sole proprietor or one-employee corporation from contributing 100 percent.

Profit Sharing Plans

Profit sharing plans allow employees to share in the company's profits, usually through an employer contribution that is a percentage of compensation. Despite what the name implies, profit sharing plans are not dependent on corporate profits for contributions to be made. Contribution levels may be changed from one year to the next. Plan participants generally do not control how the contributions are invested.

401(k) Plans

401(k) plans are defined contribution plans that are generically known as "employee thrift and savings plans." You, as an eligible employee, elect in advance to defer part of your compensation to the plan, and sometimes your employer will match some or all of it. Neither the amount deferred nor your employer-matching contribution is included in your income until distributed from the plan.

A common level of employer-matching contribution is 50 cents for every dollar the employee contributes, up to a set percentage limit. For example, your employer may contribute 3 percent of your compensation if you contribute 6 percent. Looking at this another way, it is like a guaranteed 50 percent first-year return on the amount you contribute each year.

Your own contributions are vested immediately, but your right to keep the matching contributions depends on the plan's vesting schedule. Matching contributions made after 2001 must vest either all at once after no more than three years, or at a rate of 20 percent each year starting with the second year of service. Earlier matching contributions are permitted to vest at a somewhat slower rate.

Observation: As an employee eligible for matching contributions, you should make every effort to contribute at least the amount that will entitle you to the maximum available employer-matching contribution. Putting in less is like turning your back on a raise.

As a 401(k) plan participant, you usually make your own investment decisions, usually by choosing among a variety of funds selected by your employer.

401(k) Contribution Limits. For 2001, the maximum amount that you can elect to defer to a 401(k) plan is

$10,500, subject to certain percentage limits. After 2001 the allowable contribution limits will increase considerably, as shown in the chart on page 110. If you are over 50 by the end of a year, you will be allowed to make even larger contributions. Also, contributions you can make up to the dollar maximums will not be limited by any set percentage of your compensation.

Observation: This means that you may contribute the maximum dollar amount to your 401(k) plan for a year, even if that amount is half, three-quarters, or even all of your salary for the year. This important change will be especially useful in boosting retirement savings of a second family-earner. Under previous law, the amount these lower-paid individuals could contribute was very small.

Caution: Although the law will allow 401(k) deferrals of up to 100 percent of pay beginning in 2002, this option will be available only in plans that are amended to eliminate any lower percentage of compensation limits now specified in the plan.

Example: Sarah, who is 47 years old, reenters the workforce in 2002 on a part-time basis after a child care hiatus of 15 years. Her employer maintains a 401(k) plan that Sarah is eligible to participate in after three months of service. Sarah's husband earns enough to support the family, and Sarah wants to put as much of her earnings as possible into a retirement plan on a pretax basis. Sarah expects to earn $10,000 in compensation in 2002 during the time she is eligible to make elective 401(k) deferrals. *Result:* If Sarah wishes to, she may contribute 100 percent of compensation to the plan. Only the annual dollar limit on 401(k) contributions would reduce the amount she can contribute.

Annual 401(k) Elective Deferral Limits*

Year	Under Age 50	Age 50 or Older (Includes Catch-Up)
2001	$10,500	$10,500
2002	$11,000	$12,000
2003	$12,000	$14,000
2004	$13,000	$16,000
2005	$14,000	$18,000
2006 and later	$15,000 as indexed	$20,000 as indexed

* Not more than 100 percent of compensation

Note that even though these pretax contributions will allow you to avoid immediate income tax, they are subject to Social Security tax.

Special nondiscrimination rules apply to 401(k) elective deferrals, but those rules won't limit the catch-up contributions you make if you are age 50 or over. If your employer chooses to match catch-up contributions, the matching contributions will be subject to the nondiscrimination rules that usually apply to employer-matching contributions.

For Small Employers

The savings incentive match plan for employees (SIMPLE) can be set up by companies with 100 or fewer employees that don't offer other types of retirement plans. As its name implies, a SIMPLE plan is easier and less expensive to set up and administer than a standard qualified retirement plan. Under this type of plan, employees may defer up to $6,500 for 2001. (For after 2001, see chart below.) Employers that offer a SIMPLE generally must make a nonelective or matching contribution in the 2–3 percent range on behalf of each plan participant.

The 2001 Tax Act also increased the contribution limits employees can make to SIMPLE plans, as shown in the following table.

SIMPLE Plan Maximum Deferrals*

Year	Under Age 50	Age 50 or Older (Includes Catch-Up)
2001	$6,500	$6,500
2002	$7,000	$7,500
2003	$8,000	$9,000
2004	$9,000	$10,500
2005	$10,000	$12,000
2006 and later	$10,000 as indexed	$12,500 as indexed

* Not more than 100 percent of compensation

Defined Benefit Pension Plans

Unlike a defined contribution plan, a defined benefit plan—commonly called a pension plan—pays a fixed monthly amount of income at retirement. The benefit is determined using a formula specified in the plan, usually based on your salary and the number of years you have worked for your employer. Some companies increase retirement benefits to help overcome the impact of inflation.

You are entitled to your monthly pension benefit whether or not the plan contributions have been invested well. If the value of the investments falls below the amount needed to fund the promised benefit, the employer must contribute more to the plan, so you do not bear the risk of bad investments or a severe market downturn. (If the plan ceases to exist, the Pension Benefit Guaranty Corporation pays promised benefits, up to a certain level.) Defined benefit plans generally do not require or allow employee contributions.

If you retire early, you will usually receive a reduced benefit, and if you work beyond normal retirement age, you receive an increased benefit when you begin to collect benefits.

Increase in Benefit Limit

The 2001 Tax Act increases the maximum annual benefit that a defined benefit pension plan can fund from the current amount of $140,000 in 2001 to $160,000 starting in 2002. The limit is reduced for benefits beginning before age 62 and is increased for payments beginning after age 65.

Nonqualified Deferred Compensation Plans

Nonqualified plans are an excellent way to reward individual executives or other employees without the need to treat all individuals similarly, if a company is willing to forgo current tax deductions for its contributions. (The company's deduction is delayed until the year the income is taxed to the executive.)

Observation: If you are a highly compensated employee, consider the benefits of coverage under a nonqualified plan. These plans offer the benefits of tax deferral on both the principal and income, as well as the ability to set aside larger amounts of retirement assets than do most qualified plans.

Caution: The employee is treated as a general creditor of the employer in the event that the company enters bankruptcy. This means that if your employer goes bankrupt, you have to get in line with all the other general creditors to get a portion of your employer's remaining assets.

> **Observation:** The 2001 Tax Act's future income tax rate cuts will increase the tax savings from deferred compensation plans by decreasing the amount of tax that you will owe on future plan distributions.

Under a deferred compensation plan, you elect to defer a portion of your salary or bonus until a future date (for example, retirement). To get the tax savings, you generally must agree, before the period in which compensation is earned or awarded, to defer that compensation.

Your Resources

Planning for retirement can include making contributions to Keogh plans, other self-employed retirement plans, or IRAs, and making after-tax contributions to employer plans and 401(k) plans, if they are available to you. Make sure you maximize the tax benefits by carefully considering the type of plan and whether contributions are deductible. The 2001 Tax Act broadens your opportunities to make deductible contributions.

Keogh Plans

If you are self-employed, you can maximize your retirement savings by taking advantage of self-employed retirement fund (Keogh plan) contributions. You can make a deductible contribution to your own retirement plan up to the due date (including extensions) of your return. But the plan itself must be set up by the end of the year for which the contribution is made to take advantage of the deferred payment rule.

There are three general types of Keogh plans from which to choose:

• *Profit sharing plan.* Annual contributions may be discretionary, up to a certain percentage of self-employment income.

• *Money purchase plan.* Yearly contributions based on a chosen percentage of self-employment income are mandatory.

• *Defined benefit plan.* Contributions are based on complex calculations. Although this is the most expensive kind of plan to operate, older highly compensated self-employed individuals usually find that it permits them to make the largest tax-deductible contributions.

Keogh contribution and deduction limits are the same as those for other qualified retirement plans, with adjustments for the way the self-employed's earned income is figured.

 Observation: If you are self-employed and have employees, you must remember that Keogh plans are subject to complex nondiscrimination and coverage rules. You generally can't cover just yourself if you have half-time or full-time employees over the age of 21 who have worked for you for a year or more.

Simplified Employee Pension Plans

If you are self-employed or have a small company, you can also choose to use this IRA-type plan, in which a percentage of net self-employment income is contributed to the plan (similar to a defined contribution Keogh plan). Unlike Keogh plans, SEPs can be established as late as the extended tax return due date for the prior tax year. SEPs must also provide comparable benefits for employees who satisfy certain liberal eligibility requirements. While simpler to administer than regular Keogh plans, SEPs provide fewer options than Keogh plans do for accumulating large retirement benefits.

Traditional and Roth IRAs

Any person under age 70½ (or older for Roth IRAs) with $2,000 of earned income during the year can establish an IRA. There are two very different types of IRAs (more detail concerning each type follows below):

• *Traditional IRAs.* Contributions are deductible if the IRA owner is not covered by a qualified retirement plan or if income requirements are met; distributions are fully or partly taxable. Nondeductible contributions may be made by those whose income level is too high to take deductions for these contributions.
• *Roth IRAs.* If you meet the income requirements (described below) to make Roth IRA contributions, you should seriously consider doing so. Roth IRAs are an excellent retirement vehicle. While contributions are not deductible, earnings paid to you from these accounts are tax-free as long as certain re-

quirements are met. Generally, the account must exist for at least five tax years, and you must receive the funds after you've reached age 59½, or as a result of death or disability, or for certain first-time home purchases (limited to $10,000).

The maximum amount that you can give to a Roth IRA for a year phases out over an AGI range of $95,000–$110,000 for singles, and $150,000–$160,000 for married joint-return filers. If you are not above these income levels, you may make a contribution even if you participate in an employer-sponsored retirement plan. If your income is above these levels, you are ineligible to contribute to a Roth IRA.

Higher Contribution Limits

The 2001 Tax Act increased the maximum annual IRA contribution limit beginning in 2002 and permits extra catch-up contributions if you are 50 or older as of the end of a year. The higher limit applies to both traditional and Roth IRAs.

Increased IRA Contribution Limits

Year	Regular Contribution	Catch-Up Contribution
2001	$2,000	$0
2002	$3,000	$500
2003	$3,000	$500
2004	$3,000	$500
2005	$4,000	$500
2006	$4,000	$1,000
2007	$4,000	$1,000
2008 and later	$5,000	$1,000

Observation: The increase in maximum IRA contributions gives you greater opportunities to save for retirement on a tax-favored basis and will help you to rely less on employer retirement plans and Social Security. Over many years, the added savings made possible by the 2001 Tax Act can add up.

Observation: The 2001 Tax Act does not increase the income limits that apply to deductible IRAs, eligibility for a Roth IRA, or conversion of a traditional IRA to a Roth IRA. So if you are a high-income tax payer, the only benefit you receive from the IRA changes is the ability to make modestly larger contributions to nondeductible regular IRAs.

Traditional IRAs

Your ability to make tax deductible contributions to a traditional IRA is limited by your income level if you are an active participant in your employer-sponsored retirement plan. The maximum deductible contribution you can make phases out over the following income levels:

Phase-Out of IRA Deductions for Employer Plan Participants

Year	Singles and Heads of Households		Marrieds Filing Joint Returns	
	Full Deduction	No Deduction	Full Deduction	No Deduction
2001	$33,000	$43,000	$53,000	$63,000
2002	$34,000	$44,000	$54,000	$64,000
2003	$40,000	$50,000	$60,000	$70,000
2004	$45,000	$55,000	$65,000	$75,000
2005	$50,000	$60,000	$70,000	$80,000
2006	$50,000	$60,000	$75,000	$85,000
2007 and later	$50,000	$60,000	$80,000	$100,000

If you are married, but you and your spouse file separately, your deduction phase-out range is from zero to $10,000 of adjusted gross income (AGI), effectively preventing each of you from taking IRA deductions in almost all cases in which at least one spouse is an active participant in an employer-sponsored retirement plan.

A nonworking spouse or a working spouse who is not a participant in a qualified retirement plan, but whose spouse is, may make tax deductible contributions to a regular IRA on a joint return even though the working spouse is an active retirement plan participant. The availability of this deduction phases out for couples with an AGI between $150,000 and $160,000.

> **Observation:** If you qualify, you should always make a contribution to a Roth IRA rather than making a nondeductible contribution to a traditional IRA. No deduction is allowed in either case, but the money you earn on the nondeductible traditional IRA contributions will be taxed to you when you receive it, whereas there is the potential for completely tax-free distributions from the Roth IRA.

Conversions to Roth IRAs

Preexisting IRAs may be converted into Roth IRAs if your income is less than $100,000 (regardless of whether you are single or married). You'll have to pay income tax on these conversions, but not the 10 percent penalty that applies to early withdrawals. Money distributed from a Roth IRA within five years of the conversion that comes from converted amounts will be subject to the 10 percent penalty tax. You can change your mind and undo a conversion from a traditional IRA to a Roth IRA by transferring the funds back to a regular IRA in a direct trustee-to-trustee transfer. This will eliminate the tax liability from the conversion. You might need to do this, for example, if your AGI for the conversion year exceeds the $100,000 income limit, making you ineligible to convert. Or you may want to switch back if the value of the assets in the Roth IRA has dropped, and you don't want to pay tax on the conversion based on the higher value of the assets on the conversion date. If you converted to a Roth IRA in 2001, you will have until October 15, 2002, to transfer it back to a traditional IRA, assuming you have filed a timely 2001 tax return, including extensions. If you filed your return before undoing the conversion, you'll need to file an amended return to report the reversal and eliminate your tax liability from the conversion.

If you have switched back to a regular IRA from a Roth IRA, you can reconvert to another Roth IRA and have your tax liability figured on the basis of the later conversion. However, you cannot reconvert until the start of the year after the original Roth IRA conversion was made, or, if later, more than 30 days after you switched the Roth IRA back to a traditional IRA.

Example: John converted a $100,000 IRA brokerage account (to which he had made only deductible contributions) to a Roth IRA in January 2001, giving him $100,000 of taxable income on the conversion. If the value of that Roth IRA account fell to $70,000 in April 2002, John would nonetheless be liable for tax on $100,000. However, if he transfers the $70,000 directly back to a traditional IRA, he will wipe out his tax liability from the conversion. Then he can reconvert to another Roth IRA after the waiting period has passed (explained above), perhaps before the value of the assets in the traditional IRA has fully recovered.

Observation: When it comes to IRAs, the earlier contributions are made, the better. Take the case of a 22-year-old who contributes $2,000 annually to an IRA for just 10 years, stopping after age 31. Assuming an annual growth rate of 10 percent, the assets in that IRA will increase to approximately $895,000 by the time the IRA owner is 65 years old, even though he has contributed only $20,000 to the account.

Contrast that with a person who waits until age 32 to start contributing to an IRA, but contributes $2,000 for 33 years. The funds also earn 10 percent, but at age 65 this person's account balance is only about $540,000—that is $355,000 less than the person who started contributing at age 22, despite $46,000 more in contributions.

As is made clear above, once you establish the retirement savings vehicle or vehicles that are in line with your goals (and, obviously, for which you are eligible and which are available to you), you should contribute early and regularly to benefit more fully from the effects of tax-free compounding.

Observation: You do not have to wait until you are sure of your income for a year to contribute to an IRA. You can give to either a regular IRA or a Roth IRA at any time and switch accounts by October 15 of the following year (if you have extended your tax return due date until then). For example, if you make a Roth IRA contribution or conversion during 2001 and it turns out that your income for that year is more than the allowable limit, you can transfer the funds and their earnings to a regular IRA (deductible or nondeductible, depending upon your circumstances).

Observation: Because many people in their teens and early twenties do not earn enough to save on a regular basis, this is an excellent opportunity for parents and grandparents to give their children and grandchildren a long-term gift costing a fraction of its ultimate value. If your children or grandchildren work, consider helping them set up a kiddie IRA to capitalize on the big benefits of tax-deferred compounding (tax-free compounding with a Roth IRA) over long periods of time. It is amazing how much the investment can grow if a contribution is made to a tax-favored retirement plan early in life. For example, if you contributed $2,000 per year for your child or grandchild while she was age 16 through 22, and never contributed another dime, assuming a 10 percent growth rate, she would have a retirement fund at age 65 of about $1.2 million, with only $14,000 in total contributions.

Observation: Giving funds to a Roth IRA for a child or grandchild will also allow the child or grandchild to withdraw $10,000 of earnings tax- and penalty-free to put toward the purchase of a first home.

New Tax Credit for Retirement Saving

The 2001 Tax Act gives those with modest incomes another reason to save for their retirement. For 2002 through 2006, a new nonrefundable tax credit is available to certain lower-income individuals who contribute to qualified retirement plans and IRAs. The maximum annual contribution eligible for the credit is $2,000, and the credit is in addition to any deduction available.

For the lowest-income individuals (up to an AGI of $30,000 for joint-return filers; $22,500 for heads of households; $15,000 for all others), the credit is 50 percent of the eligible contribution. That would be a $1,000 tax credit for a $2,000 contribution. The credit rate phases down from 50 percent to 10 percent of the contribution as AGI increases. It is totally phased out for those with an AGI above $50,000 for joint filers, $37,500 for heads of households, and $25,000 for singles. This credit is not available to students, taxpayers under 18, or dependents.

Observation: This credit will be available to many young taxpayers who are out of school but whose salaries are still modest. Be sure to tell your children about the new credit and encourage or help them to get started on their retirement saving.

Charitable Remainder Trusts

Another vehicle to consider for funding a portion of your retirement is a charitable remainder trust. Although complex rules apply, funding such trusts with appreciated securities can provide an alternative to traditional qualified and nonqualified plans because they allow you to improve your cash flow on a pretax basis.

Tax Deferred Annuities

If you have made the maximum permitted 401(k) or 403(b) contribution, contributed to an IRA, and have a decent portfolio of stocks designed to take advantage of favorable capital gains rates when the stocks are ultimately sold, you may want to consider a tax deferred annuity. The investment earnings (usually from name-brand mutual funds and other investment alternatives) can compound tax deferred within the annuity vehicle until they are withdrawn. It is important to remember that annuities will ultimately be taxed at ordinary income tax rates (not capital gains tax rates) when distributed to you, just like a traditional IRA, even if the money is invested in mutual funds that would have been taxed at a 20 percent or 18 percent rate if held outside the annuity. You should examine the expenses and fees charged by the insurance company issuing the annuity to ensure that they are competitive with other investments.

Universal Variable Life Insurance

Instead of a tax deferred annuity that will be taxed upon withdrawal, think about universal variable life insurance. Like its cousin, the tax deferred annuity, the universal variable life insurance policy has an investment component consisting of mutual funds or other investment choices. The investment earnings compound on a tax deferred basis within the life insurance policy until they are withdrawn. One benefit is that you can borrow the investment earnings tax-free. At death, unborrowed earnings are added to the face value of the policy and can be paid to beneficiaries on a tax-free basis. You should examine the expenses and fees charged by the insurance company issuing the policy to ensure that they are competitive with similar investments.

Professional Retirement Services

Beginning in 2002, the 2001 Tax Act allows you and your spouse to take advantage of tax-free retirement services from your employer. For the first time, this service can be provided by your employer as a non-taxable fringe benefit.

Observation: Retirement planning has become a very complicated, difficult process involving important income tax, investing, estate planning, and other family-related issues. This nontaxable fringe benefit should give you better access to professionals who can help you choose the right tools and make the right decisions when considering the complex options and opportunities now available when planning for your retirement.

Social Security

If you receive Social Security payments, you may be taxed on some of the payments you receive. Benefits must be included in income if your modified AGI (which generally includes AGI, tax-exempt interest, and certain foreign-source income with other minor adjustments) plus one-half of your Social Security benefits exceeds a certain base amount, as discussed below. The base amount begins at $25,000 for single individuals and $32,000 for married couples filing jointly. The amount of benefits included in taxable income is the lesser of one-half of benefits received or one-half of the excess of modified AGI plus 50 percent of benefits received over the base amount. A second threshold of $34,000 for singles and $44,000 for joint returns results in more of your benefits being taxable. If this threshold is exceeded, you must include the lesser of 85 percent of benefits or the sum of the lesser of the amount included under the old rules or $6,000 ($4,500 for singles) plus 85 percent of the amount by which modified AGI, increased by 50 percent of Social Security benefits, exceeds $44,000 ($34,000 for single individuals).

Observation: The calculation of taxable Social Security benefits is not a simple one. It is often loosely stated that this provision will subject 50 or 85 percent of Social Security benefits to tax. In many cases, determining the amount of benefits actually subject to tax involves complicated calculations.

Observation: Because the second threshold for the tax on Social Security benefits for married filers is only $10,000 more than that for single filers, a substantial "marriage penalty" results. For example, an unmarried couple filing separately, each with total income of $37,000—$12,000 of which is from Social Security—would each be taxed on $3,000 of their Social Security benefits. If they were married filing jointly, however, $20,400 of their Social Security benefits would be taxed.

Observation: The Social Security Administration now sends annual statements detailing an individual's earnings, contributions, and estimated future benefits. If you haven't received these benefit statements, use Form SSA-7004, Request for Earnings and Benefit Estimate Statement, to obtain a listing of your lifetime earnings and an estimate of your Social Security benefit. There is a limited period of time in which to correct mistakes.

 Observation: The earnings limit, which previously reduced Social Security benefits by $1 for every $3 that benefits recipients age 65 through 69 earned over a certain limit, has been repealed. As a result, those who work beyond age 65 no longer have their benefits reduced. However, earnings limits still apply to those below age 65 (see Chapter 10).

Web Site

To get information about the Social Security system, see http://www.ssa.gov, the Social Security Administration Web site.

Required Retirement Plan Distributions

You must begin to take at least a specified minimum amount of distributions from your qualified plans and traditional IRAs by April 1 of the year after the year you turn 70½. If you are still working at that time and you aren't at least a 5 percent owner of your company, you can defer minimum distributions from a company retirement plan (but not an IRA) until April 1 of the year after you retire. If you don't take the minimum distribution, you will have to pay a 50 percent excise tax. Obviously, this is something to try to avoid.

Observation: Minimum distributions are not required from Roth IRAs during the life of the owner. This allows the tax advantages of Roth IRAs to continue until the Roth IRA owner's death and allows the income tax-free benefits to be passed to a spouse or other family member.

Before 2001, the amount you were required to take out of your retirement plan each year—known as the "required minimum distribution"—was based on a variety of complex factors. You could figure required distributions based on your own life expectancy or on the joint life expectancy of you and your designated beneficiary, which decreased the amount of required distributions. By the required beginning date—which depended on the type of plan—you also had to decide whether you were going to use the term-certain method or the annual recalculation method to figure your distributions. The whole process was very complicated and had many pitfalls that trapped unwary retirees, often causing unfavorable tax results.

After taking years of criticism, the IRS proposed new rules that plan members can use to figure their required distributions for 2001, no matter which method they used before. Similar rules will apply for 2002 and later years. The new rules are simpler, generally spread pay-outs over a longer time, and give you more flexibility in naming and changing beneficiaries.

Under the new method, you figure your required distribution simply by dividing your account balance at the end of the previous year by a factor for your age that comes from an IRS table that is available from your employer or the IRS. You use the same factor whether or not you have named a beneficiary, and if so, no matter how old the beneficiary is. (The only exception is if you have named your spouse as your beneficiary and he or she is more than 10 years younger than you.) Required distributions under the new method are almost always smaller than under the old system.

Caution: Make sure your 2001 minimum IRA distribution is figured using the new rules. For most people, the amount that must be distributed to you in 2001 is much lower than the minimum distribution that would have been required using the old rules.

There also are new, more favorable rules for distributions after the account owner's death. If you have named a beneficiary, the remaining amounts in the account are distributed over the beneficiary's remaining life expectancy. The required distribution period is determined by reference to the beneficiary on December 31 following death. Through post-death planning such as disclaimers or estate distributions or settlement, the post-death distribution deferral can be maximized. If your surviving spouse is the sole beneficiary of your IRA, he or she is allowed to treat it as his or her own and name his or her own beneficiaries. However, that's generally not the case if the IRA is held in trust for your spouse.

Observation: Beneficiary designation planning can provide children or grandchildren with substantial funds for tax deferred compounding during their lifetimes.

Observation: If you continue to work past age 70½, you can hold off taking distributions from retirement accounts, but not regular IRAs, until your actual retirement date, as long as you are not a 5 percent owner of the business for which the plan was established.

Observation: Roth IRAs are exempt from the rules requiring distributions to begin at age 70½. Tax-free buildup can continue within a Roth IRA for your entire life. If you don't need the money during your lifetime, this can increase the amount of income tax free accumulations in the account to pass to children and grandchildren.

Idea Checklist

▢ Maximize participation in employer plans, especially if your employer "matches" 401(k) plan contributions. Consider contributing the maximum amount permitted.

▢ If you are 50 or older, consider making extra catch-up contributions.

▢ Make your IRA contributions at the beginning of each calendar year to maximize the tax deferred buildup.

▢ Self-employed individuals should consider which self-employment retirement plan is best for them. Remember that Keogh plans need to be established before year-end for a tax deduction, although actual contributions can be made as late as the extended tax return due date.

▢ Establish a Roth IRA for 2001 if your income level permits. This may be done even if you are in a qualified retirement plan and are not permitted to make deductible contributions to a traditional IRA. A

Roth IRA is especially desirable if you want to avoid making lifetime distributions required by traditional IRAs. Traditional IRAs have detailed distribution requirements.

☐ Consider whether converting a preexisting IRA to a Roth IRA makes sense for you and whether you can manage the tax liability generated from the conversion.

☐ Fund a Roth or other IRA for children and grandchildren who have earnings but insufficient cash flow to contribute to their own retirement plans.

☐ A charitable remainder trust can improve retirement cash flow if funded with highly appreciated assets.

☐ Review your beneficiary designations on retirement accounts to maximize the family's income-deferral opportunities.

When it comes to retirement, the premise of the new tax law is that Americans should have the financial freedom to be relatively independent in their later years. Whether all taxpayers are financially able as well as willing to make the change is another matter. This book is an effort to smooth the learning curve for everybody. These retirement planning suggestions and techniques are not universally applicable, of course; each person must pick and choose among them depending on individual circumstances. But as we have seen, the government is providing more tax help for retirement saving, and the tax breaks stretch across the income spectrum. The tax cut of 2001 truly offers something for everyone.

We turn next to the law's effects on home owner-ship. Most people do not give much thought to the federal tax implications of owning a home. They know they can deduct mortgage interest and real es-tate taxes, but, in fact, many other aspects of owning a home have tax consequences.

Tax Advantages of Home Ownership

Real estate ownership is usually a sign of wealth, and with wealth usually comes higher federal income tax. But property ownership carries with it many special tax advantages. This chapter will take up the tax considerations of home ownership in detail and explain how to use the Tax Code provisions to minimize federal tax bills. For instance, a home office has become easier to claim as a deduction. A vacation home may be rented to a tenant, though the rules on how to treat rental fees and expenses need careful study. Interest on limited amounts of home-equity loans is fully deductible for ordinary income tax calculations, however the proceeds are used. But when calculating the Alternative Minimum Tax (AMT), if the loan proceeds are not used for investment purposes, one can deduct home-equity loan interest to the extent that the loan was used to improve the house. "Points" paid to secure mortgages from a bank or other lender may be treated in several ways. Finally, there are special tax breaks on gains incurred when selling a house.

The 2001 Tax Act will have some interesting effects on home owners' finances as the changes are phased in over the next decade.

For instance, millions of taxpayers may stop itemizing deductions as the standard deduction for couples gradually rises. By 2010, the standard deduction will exceed the total deductions that many people could claim by itemizing. Home owners should not complain if this happens to them since their total taxes will decline and their tax situation will be simplified. Some may choose to sell their homes and rent, using the freed capital for other investments. At the same time, people who already rent out their homes will benefit from lower tax rates on their rental income.

Home owners who continue to itemize will find their deductions worth slightly less than before because tax rates will be lower. This will be particularly true for those who benefit by dropping out of the 27.5 percent bracket as the upper limit of the 15 percent bracket is raised.

The material that follows describes techniques and tools that will help you maximize the tax benefits of owning a home.

Tax Benefits of Owning a Home

Interest Deduction

Generally, you can deduct interest that is paid during the tax year on several types of debt related to your home or on home-equity loans, as long as they are secured by a qualified residence (your principal residence and one other home).

Mortgage Interest

You can deduct interest on debt that is incurred in acquiring, constructing, or substantially improving a qualified residence. Together, these are referred to as "acquisition indebtedness." The combined amount of debt that can be considered acquisition indebtedness is capped at $1 million.

 Observation: Debt on a maximum of two residences can be counted toward the $1 million limit. Thus, if you have a city home, a beach home, and a mountain home, only debt related to your principal residence and one of the other residences can qualify as home acquisition indebtedness.

Observation: If you are thinking about the purchase of a second or third home and you already have $1 million of acquisition indebtedness, consider using a trust to purchase the property, with your children as trust beneficiaries. The trust can rent the property to you at fair market value rates. In other words, if you've used this up either on your first home or on your first and second homes in aggregate, and you're looking to purchase another home, the trust option is a good one from a tax perspective.

Margin interest cannot qualify as mortgage interest even where you borrow from your brokerage account to purchase a residence, since margin debt cannot qualify as mortgage debt because it is secured by the assets in your account, not by the purchased home.

Home-Equity Loans

Interest is deductible on up to $100,000 of home-equity loans. For the interest to be deductible, the home-equity loan cannot exceed the fair market value of the residence, reduced by any acquisition indebtedness.

The reason for securing a home-equity loan is generally not relevant when determining whether interest paid on it is deductible. For example, the fact that the proceeds from a home-equity loan are used to finance personal consumption, such as the purchase of a new car or paying college expenses, does not affect interest deductibility.

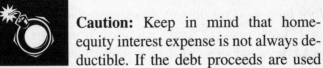 **Observation:** Consider refinancing non-deductible personal expenditures, such as an auto loan or credit card debt, with a home-equity loan. If the tax savings from the interest deduction are used to further pay down the principal portion of the loan, the debt will be paid off sooner.

Caution: Keep in mind that home-equity interest expense is not always deductible. If the debt proceeds are used to purchase municipal bonds, for example, the interest expense is not deductible.

Vacation Homes

If your vacation home is a "residence," the mortgage interest you pay is generally deductible. If your vacation home is partly your residence and partly a rental property (see below), your interest deduction must be prorated, along with your other expenses.

A vacation home is generally considered a residence if you use it for personal purposes for more than the greater of 14 days per year or 10 percent of the number of days the home is rented out at a fair rental value. Personal use is use by you or a co-owner of the property, or a family member of either, and use by other people who do not pay a fair market rental. Days when you are performing maintenance and repairs on a vacation property are not considered personal-use days. If you own a vacation home and rent it out to others, the term of the rental will affect the tax treatment of rental income.

• *More than 14 days personal use/rented fewer than 15 days.* If you rent out a home for 14 days per year or less, it may qualify as a second residence. Any rental income is tax-free, and any rental expenses are not deductible (except mortgage interest and real estate taxes).

• *More than 14 days personal use/rented more than 14 days.* If you rent out your vacation home for more than 14 days per year, and your personal use exceeds the greater of 14 days or 10 percent of the rental period, the home is a personal residence subject to the vacation home rules. You can deduct a proportionate share of property taxes and interest attributable to your personal use. The rental income can be reduced by the balance of the interest and taxes. In addition, you can deduct depreciation and other operating expenses attributable to the rental to the extent of any remaining rental income. Note that you cannot claim expenses in excess of the rental income.

• *Fewer than 15 days personal use/rented more than 14 days.* If you rent your home for more than 14 days and your personal use does not exceed the greater of 14 days or 10 percent of the rental period, the vacation home is considered a rental property. Interest and taxes are allocated between personal and rental use of the property. In addition, other expenses allocable to the rental activity can be considered in full, even if this results in a loss. The loss, however, will be subject to the passive activity rules discussed in Chapter 2 and generally will be deductible only to the extent of passive activity income. Interest allocated to your personal use of the home is personal interest and may not be deductible because the home generally is not considered a "residence."

Rental Properties

If your vacation home is fully rented without any personal use, it will be considered a rental property and will not be subject to the special vacation home rules. As a rental property, taxes, interest, and other expenses are deductible, subject to the passive activity loss rules. However, up to $25,000 of passive rental real estate losses can be deducted each year against other income such as compensation, interest, and dividends, if the owner meets certain "active participation" requirements. The $25,000 exception begins to phase out for home owners with an AGI over $100,000 and is fully phased out for home owners with an AGI over $150,000.

Home Office Deduction

Home is where the office is for a growing number of consultants, entrepreneurs, and telecommuters. Although expenses associated with use of a residence are generally not deductible, a home office deduction is permitted for certain expenses if a portion of the home is used exclusively and on a regular basis as the principal place of business or as a place to meet or deal with customers or clients in the ordinary course of the home owner's trade or business.

In addition, home office deductions are available to home owners who use a separate structure that is nearby, but not attached to the home, regularly and exclusively in connection with their trade or business.

Exclusive and Regular Use

To meet the exclusive-use requirement, you as the home owner must use a portion of the residence *solely* for conducting business. There is no provision for *de minimis* personal use, such as typing a personal letter or making a personal phone call. If you are employed by a company, your use of the home office must be "for the convenience of the employer."

Principal Place of Business

Until a couple of years ago, "principal place of business" was defined very restrictively for purposes of the home office deduction, preventing many who worked from their homes from claiming deductions. However, a tax law change that went into effect in 1999 opened up the deduction to many more home office users. In addition to the place where the central functions of a business are performed, the term "principal place of business" now includes areas used for a business's administrative or management activities, if there is no other fixed location where the home owner conducts these activities. This is the case even if most of the other work of the business is done outside of the home office. So, for example, it will be easier for salespeople, tradespeople, and manufacturer's representatives who work out of their homes, but perform much of their work at their customers' locations, to claim home office deductions. Here again, if you are an employee, use of your home must be for your employer's convenience to claim a home office deduction.

More people who work at home will be able to take a home office deduction. Typical expenses include a portion of rent, depreciation, repairs, and utilities.

Observation: Under this new definition of principal place of business, more individuals will also be able to deduct the cost of traveling to and from their home (as their principal place of business) to other business locations. In the past, these transportation costs were considered nondeductible commuting expenses.

Observation: The rules about the home office deductions are still complex. A separate tax form is required with Form 1040 to claim the deduction. (Self-employed individuals claim home office expenses on Form 8829 and on Schedule C; employees use Form 2106 or Form 2106EZ and claim them as miscellaneous itemized deductions on Schedule A Form 1040, subject to the 2 percent of the AGI floor.)

Another consideration in evaluating whether it makes sense to take the deductions is that the portion of the home for which home office deductions are claimed may not qualify for the home sale exclusion.

Personal Residence Trust

A first or second home is an ideal asset to transfer to a personal residence trust—a popular gift tax planning technique (see Chapter 6). In this case, the property is transferred to the trust for a period of years, during which you retain the right to live in or use the property. At the end of the term, the property passes to whomever you choose, either in further trust or outright. The value of the transfer is discounted for gift tax purposes because of your retained right to live in the residence. In addition, all future appreciation in the value of the home is transferred free of gift tax.

Although your beneficiaries will own the residence (either in trust or outright) at the end of the trust term, you can lease the property from them at a fair rental value. If you die before the end of the trust term, the property remains in your estate. Consequently, the retained right to live in the property or to use it should be for a reasonable period given your age and general health.

 Observation: The personal residence trust's governing instrument (the document that creates and "rules" the trust) must prohibit the trust from selling or transferring the residence, directly or indirectly, to you, your spouse, or an entity controlled by you or your spouse, during the time in which the trust is a grantor trust (a trust in which the grantor keeps some interests and control and therefore is taxed on any income from the trust). This means that the grantors will not be able to get the basis step-up at death if they live beyond the trust term. This makes a personal residence trust less attractive for homes that are already highly appreciated.

Home Sales

Principal Residence Gain Exclusion

As a home seller, you may exclude up to $250,000 of gain from the sale of your home as long as it is owned and used by you as your principal residence for at least two of the five years before the sale. Qualifying married taxpayers filing jointly may exclude up to $500,000. The full exclusion is not available if, within the two-year period before the sale, you sold another home for which you claimed the exclusion.

Qualifying for the $500,000 Exclusion. A married couple filing jointly may exclude up to $500,000 of gain from the sale of their home if:

- either spouse owned the home for at least two of the five years preceding the sale;
- both spouses used the home for at least two of the five years preceding the sale;
- neither spouse sold another home at a gain within the previous two years and excluded all or part of that gain using the exclusion.

Partial Exclusion. A partial exclusion may be available if you do not meet the two-year ownership and use requirement, or sell your home within two years of a previous home sale for which you used the exclusion. If you fail to meet either requirement because of a change in employment, health, or other unforeseen circumstances, the exclusion is based on the ratio of qualifying months to 24 months (or, if less, on the ratio of the number of months between the sale date of a previous home for which the exclusion was claimed and the sale date of the current home to 24 months).

For example, suppose a single person owned and used a home as a principal residence for one year (and did not previously use the exclusion on another home sale within the previous two years) and must move for job-related reasons. The partial exclusion rule allows this person to exclude up to $125,000 of his or her gain from the sale of the residence ($250,000 exclusion times 12 divided by 24).

Partial Exclusion Rule for Joint Filers. If a married couple filing jointly doesn't meet all the conditions for claiming an exclusion of up to $500,000, the gain that is excluded on the home sale is the sum of the exclusion each spouse would be entitled to if both were single. For this purpose each spouse is treated as owning the home for the period that either spouse owned the home.

For example, a couple sells a home that one spouse owned and used as a principal residence for 10 years and the other spouse used as a principal residence for only one year. They sell the home because of illness. They may exclude up to $375,000 of profit from the sale ($250,000 for one spouse, plus $125,000 for the other spouse).

Observation: Special care and planning is needed to preserve the full home sale exclusion in divorce situations.

> **Observation:** Home sellers in hot, up-scale real estate markets will have to pay capital gains tax on any profit above the $250,000/$500,000 limits. The rollover break that used to defer unlimited amounts of home sale gain, provided an equally expensive residence was purchased as a replacement, is no longer available. Since the new exclusion is available once every two years regardless of whether it's been used before, some home owners may decide to sell before their gains exceed the limits. Then additional gain on their replacement residence could also qualify for the exclusion in another two years.

> **Observation:** Because a vacation home is not your principal residence, it does not qualify for the tax-free treatment when it is sold. A residence that you also use as a vacation home can't be swapped tax free for another property in a like-kind exchange.

Home Purchases

Real Estate Taxes

In general, real estate taxes can be deducted. In the year of a home sale, however, the Tax Code requires the deduction for real estate taxes to be apportioned between the buyer and seller according to the number of days each held the property during the year. It does not matter that your sales contract contains a different division of responsibility for the taxes.

 Observation: Even though the buyer or seller might pay the entire tax, the deduction is limited by the statutory formula.

 Observation: You will need your closing statement from a home sale or purchase to calculate the amount of deductible real estate taxes. You will also need to know whether the states in which you purchased or sold a home require prepayment of real estate taxes or whether such taxes are paid in arrears.

Mortgage Points

Mortgage "points" incurred with a home loan are usually significant. A point is a charge paid by a borrower for taking out a loan, in which each point is 1 percent of the loan amount. You must amortize most points over the life of the loan; however, you can deduct points you pay for acquiring or making improvements to your main residence in the year paid. The deductibility of points depends on whether the lender assesses them as additional interest or as a service charge. This is sometimes a difficult determination. Points are generally considered additional interest if the lender is charging for the use of money. If points are assessed for application preparation or processing, they are treated as a service charge and added to the purchaser's basis in the residence and thus are nondeductible.

 Observation: Do not assume you should pay points when purchasing a new home. Think about how long you are likely to own the property. If you expect to sell the property within five years or less, it may be more advantageous to pay a slightly higher interest rate to get a no-points or low-points mortgage loan.

Points may be deducted in full during the year they were paid if the following requirements are met:

1. Points are paid directly to the lender by the borrower; points are treated as paid directly to the lender if the borrower provides unborrowed funds at least equal to the points charged at the closing or as a down payment or escrow deposit.

2. The loan is incurred for the purchase or improvement of a principal residence.

3. Points are an established business practice in the area in which the loan originates. In other words, banks and other lending institutions in that geographical area typically impose points when granting mortgage loans.

4. The dollar amount of the points is typical for the area in which the loan originates.

5. The points are clearly designated as such on the settlement form.

6. The points are expressed as a percentage of the loan amount.

Borrowers who do not satisfy these requirements must amortize the points over the life of the loan.

 Observation: The most common situations in which points must be amortized include the purchase of a second residence and refinancing the principal home's mortgage.

 Observation: The unamortized points remaining when an underlying mortgage is paid off after a sale or refinancing are deductible in full.

Idea Checklist

☐ Convert nondeductible interest expense into tax deductible home-equity interest expense.

☐ Know the vacation home rules before renting out your second home.

☐ Consider placing a principal residence or second home in a personal residence trust.

☐ Review closing documents from real estate sales

or purchases to find deductible real estate tax amounts.

□ If you refinanced your home during 2001, any remaining unamortized points on the paid-off loan are fully deductible on your 2001 return.

Owning a home is a cornerstone of the American Dream, and a home has almost always been most taxpayers' most valuable asset, both financially and emotionally. The tax law gives home ownership the numerous opportunities that this chapter has described.

The next chapter takes up saving for education—a high priority in the new tax law. In the past, many of the Tax Code's incentives for education savings were not available to taxpayers in the higher brackets. Beginning in 2002, however, families with relatively high incomes will be permitted to put away more after-tax money and withdraw the gains tax-free, which will increase their flexibility for funding education for children and grandchildren. Let's look at that in detail.

How to Maximize Savings for Education

To pay for a child's quality education, parents will do just about anything, even spend their life savings, assume second mortgages, and work at multiple jobs if that's what's necessary. It gets harder and harder to keep up with college tuition soaring far beyond the inflation rate.

Fortunately, the Tax Code now offers some real incentives to help parents fund their children's education. This chapter describes a number of helpful tuition-financing techniques. Despite the fact that there are more available tax breaks, the best advice is to put aside as much as you can as early as you can.

Until now, many of the education tax incentives weren't available to those with higher incomes. But starting in 2002, families with higher incomes will be able to take advantage of some tax breaks, including what will become by far the best educational tax break, the much improved Section 529 plan, which has no income limits. Also starting in 2002, many of the restrictions that previously prevented taxpayers from bundling various education tax breaks together in the same year have been eliminated.

 Observation: Parents should consider the impact that Section 529 programs and Education IRAs will have on their chances of obtaining financial aid for college. Some advisers suggest that families who wish to maximize their financial aid use the types of investments that are favored in the federal financial aid formulas. These investments include retirement savings, life insurance, and home equity. There are many reasons not to engage in this type of planning:

1. The financial aid rules may change before your child is in college.

2. The favored assets under the federal formula may not be favored for your child's university-provided financial aid.

3. Most financial aid is in the form of loans, not grants—why burden yourself or your child with debt?

4. Only a small percentage of parental assets are applied to reduce each year's financial aid.

Qualified Section 529 Tuition Programs

For a number of years, the Tax Code has allowed states to set up "qualified state tuition programs," often referred to as Section 529 plans after the part of the Tax Code that authorizes them. States are permitted to offer two types of plans:

• *Prepaid tuition plans,* which allow a parent, grandparent, or other person to prepay tuition costs and certain other education expenses. Participants are generally allowed to put aside future tuition by contributing money to these plans, thus assuring tuition at today's tuition rate. These types of plans are generally available only to state residents and are meant to be used for the tuition at in-state public schools. Programs differ from state to state, however, and you have to look carefully at the details of your own state's plan. Under current federal financial aid guidelines, these plans reduce your child's financial aid dollar for dollar.

• *Tuition savings plans,* which offer more flexibility on contribution limits and investment choices, are not limited to use for attendance at in-state schools. These plans are treated as any other parental asset under federal financial aid guidelines.

As good as Section 529 state tuition programs were in the past, they will be vastly better starting in 2002. Previously, earnings on prepaid amounts were tax deferred until used to pay for the student's higher education. At that time, distributed earnings were taxable to the student-beneficiary, who was usually in a lower tax bracket than the parent or other contributor. The educational fund built up faster, owing to tax deferral, and the tax that was ultimately owed was almost always much lower than it would have been at the parent-contributor's rate.

Starting in 2002, distributions from these state tuition programs that are used to pay qualifying higher-education expenses will now be completely tax-free. And there are still no income limits on who may contribute to or benefit from these plans. As a result, they are a much improved higher-education savings vehicle.

Year-end planning tip: If you're planning to use a distribution from a state tuition plan to pay expenses due before the end of 2001, consider paying the tuition from other funds and repaying yourself with a distribution from the plan taken at the beginning of 2002. If the distribution is taken in 2001, the earnings will be taxable at the student's rate. If it's taken in 2002, it will likely be tax-free.

Also starting in 2002, private educational institutions will be permitted to establish prepaid tuition programs that will have the same tax benefits as state tuition plans, with these differences:

• The private institutions will not be able to offer savings plans.
• Distributions from these private tuition plans won't be tax-free until after 2003.

Despite these limitations, the private plans should be attractive to many parents and future students, especially to families with a history of attendance at a particular private college. It is expected that some institutions will join together to form plans that will allow students-beneficiaries to use the prepaid tuition credits at any of the member institutions. Also, tuition credits will be permitted to be rolled over from one plan to another as often as once a year. This should provide you with more flexibility if you aren't sure where your children will end up going to college. This rollover option also will be extended to state tuition plans, making them much more useful and flexible. For example, the rollover option will allow transfers between the tuition plans of different states, between a state's prepaid tuition plan and its savings plan, or between a state tuition plan and a private plan.

What Expenses Qualify?

Tax-free qualified tuition plan benefits (both state and private) will be available for tuition, fees, books, and supplies. Most room and board expenses for students who attend school at least half-time will also qualify. To figure the amount that can be received tax-free, expenses that would otherwise qualify must be reduced by tax-free scholarship grants, veterans' benefits, tax-free employer-paid educational expenses, and amounts that qualify for higher-education tax credits. Also, amounts received tax-free from a qualified tuition plan will reduce the amount of education expenses that qualify for the new tuition deduction discussed on page 174.

Distributions of earnings that exceed qualified

expenditures are taxed to the beneficiary and generally subject to a 10 percent excise tax. Amounts not used by the beneficiary can be rolled over to another beneficiary's account as long as the new beneficiary is a family member (including a spouse and, beginning in 2002, a first cousin), thus keeping the tax benefits working for other family members. Earnings not used for qualified higher-education expenses that are returned to the contributor are taxed at the contributor's rate plus the 10 percent excise tax. Earnings that are distributed on account of the beneficiary's death or disability, or on account of the beneficiary's receipt of a scholarship, are not subject to a penalty.

Observation: After 2001, the Tax Code imposes a 10 percent tax penalty for taxable distributions not used for education expenses. Previously, these plans had to impose a penalty on refunds not used for educational expenses. Each state will have to decide whether to remove its own plan's penalty for nonqualified use of funds. However, this should not be a factor in choosing a state-qualified tuition plan as long as the plan permits rollovers. If there are funds in the account that will not be used for education expenses, the account could be rolled over to a plan that does not impose a penalty of its own.

Your contributions to qualified tuition plans may be made only in cash. Unlike Coverdell Education Savings Accounts, contributors and beneficiaries are not permitted to self-direct the investments in qualified tuition plans. However, most savings plans permit an initial investment selection among different investment types, and the account owner can switch investments once every twelve months and upon any change in account beneficiaries.

Many states provide state income tax deductions for contributions to their state's qualified tuition plans.

Caution: There are a number of special rules that coordinate the benefits of various tax-favored education savings vehicles. For example, if you take distributions in the same year from a Coverdell Education Savings Account and a qualified tuition program and the cumulative distributions exceed the amount of higher-education expenses that qualify for the tax breaks, you will have to allocate the expenses between the distributions to determine how much of each can be excluded. Also, you may claim both a higher-education tax credit (assuming you otherwise qualify) and receive a tax-free distribution from a qualified tuition plan in the same year for the same student (to the extent that the distribution doesn't cover the same expenses for which the tax credit was claimed).

Gift Tax Break, Too

Payments made into qualified tuition programs are considered completed gifts at the time payment is made into the program, even though the student-beneficiary may not receive the benefit of the gift for many years. As a result, the payments are eligible for the $10,000 annual gift tax exclusion ($11,000 for 2002). In fact, five years' worth of annual-exclusion gifts can be made in one year to a qualified tuition plan. So a married couple could give $50,000 ($55,000 for 2002) each to the plan of the same beneficiary in a single year. However, no additional gifts from the couple could then be made to that beneficiary for the next four years without being subject to gift tax filings (see Chapter 6 for details).

Coverdell Education Savings Accounts

Before 2002, you could contribute up to $500 per year to Education IRAs for any child under 18. The $500 amount was phased out for contributors with modified adjusted gross income (AGI) between $95,000 and $110,000 for singles and between $150,000 and $160,000 for joint filers. Earnings are tax-free when distributed if used for qualified higher-education expenses, including tuition, fees, books, room and board, and supplies and equipment. A 6 percent excise tax was applied each year if contributions to Education IRAs for any one child exceeded $500 from all sources.

Education IRAs were recently renamed. They are now called Coverdell Education Savings Accounts (Education Savings Accounts). Beginning in 2002, the annual per-child contribution limit increases to $2,000, and the eligibility of married joint-return filers to make contributions increases to $190,000–

$220,000, double the contribution phase-out range for single contributors.

 Observation: The increase in the annual contribution limit will make Education Savings Accounts much more useful. In the past, if maximum contributions of $500 were made for a child at the beginning of each year for 18 years and they earned 7.5 percent per year, the Education IRA would have a balance of about $19,000 when the child was ready to start college. The increased contribution limit will increase that amount to about $77,000.

An even bigger change starting in 2002 is that tax-free Education Savings Account distributions can be used for kindergarten, primary-school, and secondary-school tuition and expenses as well as for higher-education expenses. Qualified expenses will include not only tuition and fees but tutoring costs, room and board, uniforms, transportation, and extended-day programs. Even some computer equipment and Internet access qualifies if used by the beneficiary and the beneficiary's family during a year that the beneficiary is enrolled in school.

Any unused amounts in an Education Savings Account must be distributed before the beneficiary turns 30 or be rolled over into an Education Savings Account for another family member under age 30. Undistributed amounts are taxed to the beneficiary at that time. Eligible family members include the beneficiary's spouse, children, brothers and sisters, and nieces and nephews. If a distribution is not used for educational expenses, the beneficiary will be taxed on the earnings and pay a 10 percent penalty.

Before 2002, the income exclusion for Education IRA distributions was not available for any year in which either HOPE Scholarship or Lifetime Learning tax credits (see page 167) were claimed. Starting in 2002, however, these breaks are available in the same year as long as expenses for which a credit is claimed aren't the same ones for which a tax-free Education Savings Account distribution is received.

Observation: Your children and grandchildren may be able to benefit from an Education Savings Account even if your income exceeds the AGI threshold. Anyone can establish an Education Savings Account for your child or grandchild. Grandparents, aunts, uncles, or even siblings can make the contributions, provided their income is below the modified AGI limitation, and the IRS agrees that even a child may contribute to his or her own Education Savings Account. Also, starting in 2002, companies will be able to make contributions to Education Savings Accounts. So if a parent's income is too high to make a contribution, his or her company may make the contribution to the child's Education Savings Account. (Such a payment would be taxable compensation to the parent, the same as if the company paid the parent who, in turn, made the contribution to the account.)

Observation: Parents who intend to send their children to private elementary and secondary schools may want to use Education Savings Accounts to help pay those costs and use qualified tuition programs to build a higher-education fund. An excise tax that used to apply if contributions were made to an Education IRA for any year that a contribution for the same beneficiary was also made to a qualified tuition plan will no longer apply beginning in 2002.

Until 2002, contributions to an Education IRA for a year must be made by the end of that calendar year. For 2002 and later years, however, you will have until April 15 of the following year to make Education Savings Account contributions.

Roth IRAs

Roth IRAs have a special distribution pay-out rule that makes them a good source of tax-advantaged cash for education funding. If you withdraw funds from a regular IRA to pay for college while you are under age 59½, the withdrawal would be mostly, if not completely, taxable. With a Roth IRA, however, you can withdraw up to the amount of your contributions tax-free for any purpose, even if you are under age 59½. Earnings on the contributions are deemed withdrawn only after you have withdrawn all contributions. If you need to withdraw earnings on the contributions to pay for qualified education expenses, they will be included in your gross income but will not be subject to the usual 10 percent early withdrawal penalty.

> **Example:** John Smith contributes $2,000 a year to a Roth IRA for 10 years. At the end of that period, he can withdraw his $20,000 cumulative contribution both income tax and penalty free. Earnings on the contributions remain in the account to further compound for his retirement.

 Observation: The increased IRA contribution limits that apply beginning in 2002 (see Chapter 3 for details) will make this strategy even more useful.

Traditional IRAs

Traditional IRAs are generally not as good a source for funding education expenses as the other vehicles described in this chapter because all distributions are included in income if all contributions were deductible. (If nondeductible contributions were made, part of each distribution is taxable and part is considered to be a return of capital.) However, if an IRA withdrawal is used to pay for qualified educational expenses for you or your spouse, child, or grandchild, no 10 percent early withdrawal penalty is imposed. Qualified educational expenses include tuition, fees, books, supplies, and required equipment at a postsecondary school.

Observation: This penalty exception does not apply to premature distributions from qualified retirement plans, but it does apply to simplified employee pension (SEP) plan distributions, which are treated as IRAs for this purpose.

Education Tax Credits

HOPE Scholarship and Lifetime Learning Credits

Taxpayers may be eligible to claim a nonrefundable HOPE Scholarship tax credit or a Lifetime Learning tax credit against their federal income taxes for qualified tuition and related expenses.

A HOPE Scholarship tax credit provides up to $1,500 in tax credits per student, but only for each of the first two years of at least half-time college enrollment. A Lifetime Learning tax credit is also available, providing an annual 20 percent tax credit on the first $5,000 of tuition and related expenses, for a maximum of $1,000 per year. (After 2002, the maximum Lifetime Learning credit increases to $2,000—that is, 20 percent of up to $10,000 of expenses.) The Lifetime Learning credit maximum applies per-household, not per-student, and can be claimed for yourself, your spouse, or your child. Note that only one of these credits can be claimed in any year for the expenses of a given student.

Students claimed as dependents may not take either credit on their own tax returns. Qualifying educational expenses a dependent student pays are treated as paid by the person who claims the student as a dependent for purposes of figuring that person's HOPE credit. Amounts paid to educational institutions by third parties, such as grandparents, are treated as paid by the student (and, in turn, by the student's parents if they claim the student as a dependent).

If you are above the income thresholds for these credits (availability of the credits phases out between a modified AGI of $40,000 and $50,000 for singles; $80,000 and $100,000 for married couples filing jointly), there may still be some opportunities to benefit from the credits. If you forgo claiming your student-child as a dependent, and the child has sufficient taxable income to be able to use the credit, the tax value of the credit may be more than you lose by giving up the dependency exemption. There is no restriction on the type of income that may be offset by the tax credit, so investment income would qualify.

 Observation: The higher your income, the better this trade-off is, since your ability to claim dependency deductions starts to phase out at about $200,000 of adjusted gross income and disappears completely at about $320,000 on a joint return.

U.S. Savings Bonds

You may exclude from income any interest received on a redemption of U.S. savings bonds purchased after 1989 when you were 24 or older if qualifying educational expenses for the tax year exceed the aggregate proceeds received from a redemption of bonds.

 Observation: The ability to use this provision in 2001 begins to phase out for single individuals with $55,750 of AGI and married couples with an AGI of $83,650 (for 2002, phase-outs begin at $57,600 and $86,400, respectively). The phase-out range for the interest exclusion is $15,000 for singles and $30,000 for joint-return filers. Because the income level is measured in the year the bonds are redeemed (which might be years into the future), you may not be able to take advantage of the provision if income levels are too high at that time. The interest income would then be subject to tax at ordinary rates.

If you are concerned that your income may be too high in the year of redemption, it might make more sense to invest in growth stocks. This will allow you to manage the capital gains income and you could transfer the stock to your child on a "just-in-time" basis, to be sold at reduced capital gains rates (see "Income Shifting and Capital Gains," page 172).

Example: Mr. Jones redeems series EE bonds in the amount of $2,000. Mr. Jones paid $1,200 for the bonds in 1990 and would have to recognize $800 of interest income upon the redemption. If Mr. Jones has qualifying education expenses of at least $2,000 during the tax year in which he redeems the bonds and his income is low enough, he does not have to report the interest income generated by the bond redemption. Qualifying educational expenses include tuition and fees spent for the taxpayer, the taxpayer's spouse, and dependents of the taxpayer.

Home-Equity Loans

If you need to borrow to pay college expenses, consider a home-equity loan. You can claim the loan interest as an itemized deduction, up to a maximum debt amount of $100,000. However, home-equity debt interest is not deductible for Alternative Minimum Tax purposes.

Student Loans

You may deduct up to $2,500 of interest paid on qualified education loans (loans taken out and used solely to meet higher-education expenses), which you are liable to repay, even if you don't itemize deductions. Interest on loans from relatives or other individuals can't be deducted. Before 2002, only the first 60 months of interest payments are eligible, but when loans are consolidated, the 60-month period usually begins at the time repayments are due on the most recent loan. Beginning in 2002, this 60-month limit no longer applies.

Before 2002, the student-loan interest deduction phases out at a modified AGI level between $40,000 and $55,000 for singles, and $60,000 and $75,000 for married joint-return filers. Starting in 2002, these phase-out ranges increase to $50,000–$65,000 for singles, and $100,000–$130,000 for married couples. So, many more people will be able to qualify for at least some deduction.

Observation: Despite the increases in the phase-out thresholds, many parents will be shut out of this deduction because their family income is too high. If borrowing is necessary in these situations, it usually makes sense for the student rather than the parent to take out the loan. The deduction is not available to a child for any year when the child is claimed as a dependent on the parents' tax return. However, the child is not likely to be a dependent when the loan is being repaid following graduation.

Relatives

Relatives, especially grandparents, with taxable estates (those that exceed 2001's $675,000 and 2002's $1 million estate and gift tax allowance) may be looking for methods to reduce their estates despite coming increases in the amounts that may escape estate tax (see Chapter 6). Payments of tuition made directly to an educational institution do not count against the gift tax annual exclusion amount. Thus, grandparents can write a tuition check directly to the school and still make a $10,000 tax-free gift ($11,000 starting in 2002) to their grandchildren without owing any gift tax or even reducing the amount that can be passed on free of estate tax. Even multiyear advance tuition payments may be structured to be gift tax-free.

Income Shifting and Capital Gains

As discussed in Chapter 2, the favorable capital gains tax rates make it worthwhile to consider shifting income to your children who will pay only a 10 percent (or possibly even an 8 percent, if they qualify) tax on capital gains.

Observation: If you expect to have capital gains from selling stock to pay for college or another major expense for a child age 14 or older, consider giving the asset to the child, who can then sell it. Assuming that the child is in a 15 percent tax bracket (or 10 percent in 2002 and later), the child will pay tax at the 10 percent capital gains rate (even if the asset is sold the next day) as long as the combined holding period exceeds 12 months. Keep in mind that both your purchase price and date of purchase will transfer to gift recipients.

Children or other individuals in the 10 or 15 percent bracket will pay only 8 percent tax on long-term capital gains if the property that is sold has been held for more than five years. Unlike the rule for individuals in higher tax brackets, the asset sold need not have been purchased after the year 2000 for the lower rate to apply. The recipient can turn around and sell the asset without an additional waiting period and owe only an 8 percent capital gains tax.

Observation: Remember, the gift tax may apply to gifts over $10,000 ($11,000 in 2002) from single individuals and $20,000 ($22,000 in 2002) from married couples.

Observation: To fund college or other expenses for children, consider assets that are likely to provide superior capital appreciation over the minimum five-year holding period. These assets can now be held in the child's name (in a UGMA [Uniform Gift to Minors Act] or UTMA [Uniform Transfers to Minors Act] account) or in trust (as long as the trustee has the ability to distribute capital gains) or be a gift to the child on a "just-in-time" basis, since there would be a carryover purchase price and purchase date.

Tuition Deduction

For 2002 through 2005 only, a limited amount of higher-education expenses will be deductible for itemizers and nonitemizers alike. As with most education tax breaks, those with higher incomes won't be able to claim this. A deduction of up to $3,000 is permitted for 2002 and 2003, for singles with an AGI no higher than $65,000 or married couples with income no higher than $130,000. For 2004 and 2005, the deduction limit for these income ranges increases to $4,000, and a maximum $2,000 deduction will be available for those with higher incomes of up to $80,000 for singles and $160,000 for married couples. The deduction isn't available to those who can be claimed as dependents on another person's tax return.

There are also other restrictions. The tuition deduction can't be claimed for a year if a HOPE or Lifetime Learning credit is claimed for the same student. Also, no deduction will be allowed for the part of a qualified tuition plan distribution, savings bond redemption, or Education Savings Account that represents tax-free earnings; however, the part of the distribution representing a return of capital will qualify for the deduction.

Employer Education Assistance

Many employers, especially larger ones, have benefit plans that provide up to $5,250 a year of education assistance to employees. This benefit is tax-free to employees if it applies to tuition and related expenses, such as fees, books, and certain associated supplies and equipment. Other related expenses, such as meals, lodging, and transportation, aren't covered by the income exclusion. The courses do not have to be job-related for the benefit to be tax-free. So, for example, a person who works as a clerk or secretary at a company could take courses toward a degree in literature, history, or economics and receive tax-free benefits. However, tax-free assistance is not available for courses involving sports, games, or hobbies.

Before 2002, education assistance plan benefits aren't available for graduate-level courses. But beginning in 2002 that restriction has been removed, making this an even more flexible education-funding device. As a result, an employee whose employer's plan permits it could receive tax-free benefits to attend graduate school part-time while working.

Tax-free benefits are not available to companies whose education assistance plan discriminates in favor of highly compensated employees and their dependents. However, union employees don't have to be covered if education assistance was the subject of good-faith bargaining.

If your employer doesn't have an education assistance plan, but reimburses you for education expenses, the reimbursement is tax-free if the education is job-related, that is, if it maintains or improves a skill currently used in your trade or business or is required to continue your employment. However, the courses can't qualify you for a new profession (such as law school courses taken by a C.P.A. or M.B.A.) or be needed for you to meet the minimum educational requirements for your current position.

If you pay for job-related courses on your own, without being reimbursed by your employer, you can deduct the expenses on your own tax return as miscellaneous itemized deductions. However, your expenses won't be fully deductible because you can only claim otherwise deductible miscellaneous expenses that exceed 2 percent of your adjusted gross income. If your AGI is $100,000, for example, your first $2,000 of miscellaneous expenses are nondeductible. Also, miscellaneous deductions cannot be claimed for Alternative Minimum Tax purposes.

Idea Checklist

- Fund a qualified tuition plan, especially if your income exceeds the threshold for Education Savings Accounts.
- If you qualify, fund an Education Savings Account and a qualified tuition plan if you plan to send your children to a private elementary or high school.
- Have lower-income family members establish Education Savings Accounts for children and grandchildren; alternatively, have children contribute to their own Education Savings Accounts.
- Shift capital gains income into a 10 percent (or 8 percent, if qualified) bracket by giving stock to your children or grandchildren age 14 or older.
- If loans are needed to help pay for educational expenses, first consider a home-equity loan.

- Be sure relatives know that tuition can be paid directly to an educational institution in addition to $10,000 annual exclusion gifts, and that up to five years' worth of annual exclusion gifts can be made at one time to a qualified tuition program.
- Consider funding a Roth IRA so you can withdraw your contributions tax-free and penalty free to pay for college.
- Check the new, higher-income thresholds for education tax incentives for 2002 to see if you qualify for any that you couldn't use in past years.
- Consider not claiming your child as a tax dependent if your child has enough income to benefit from a higher-education tax credit.

The 2001 Tax Act makes paying for college much more affordable for many. Parents need creative ways for turning tax burdens into tuition tamers, a need that Congress has begun responding to in the ways this chapter has described.

Less promising is the new tax law's treatment of our next topic—estate planning. Even so, our next chapter suggests at least some ways to turn this particular sow's ear into a silk purse.

Tax Breaks for Education

Type of Tax-Advantaged Arrangement	Main Features	Income Limits
Qualified tuition plans	Post-2001 (post-2003 for private plans) distributions for higher education expenses are tax-free Large gift tax-free contributions can be made Can be transferred to other family members	None
Coverdell Education Savings Accounts	Per-child contribution limits: 2001: $500 2002 and later: $2,000 Tax-free distributions for education Can be used for kindergarten through postgraduate, including school-related computer equipment purchase Broad investment choice	Contribution limit phases out between a modified AGI of $95,000–$110,000 for singles; $190,000–$220,000 for joint filers ($150,000–$160,000 for joint filers for 2001)
Education savings bond exclusion	Interest is tax-free on redemption for higher-education	Exclusion phases out for 2001 between a modified AGI of

Type of Tax-Advantaged Arrangement	Main Features	Income Limits
	expenses (but not room and board) Proceeds can be transferred to Education IRA or qualified tuition plan Child can't own bonds	$55,750–$70,750 ($57,600 and $72,600 for 2002) for singles; $83,650 and $113,650 for joint filers ($86,400 and $116,400 for 2002)
Student loan interest deduction	Up to $2,500 of student loan interest deductible, even by non-itemizers Can't be claimed by tax dependent	Maximum deduction phases out between a modified AGI for 2001 of $40,000–$55,000 for singles; $60,000–$75,000 for joint filers; for 2002: $50,000–$65,000 for singles; $100,000–$130,000 for joint filers
Tuition deduction	Available for 2002 to 2005 only Maximum $3,000 deduction for 2002 and 2003 Maximum $4,000 deduction for 2004 and 2005 Not available if higher-education tax credit is claimed for the same student	For 2002 and 2003, only available for singles with a modified AGI of up to $65,000 ($130,000 for joint filers). For 2004 and 2005, $2,000 deduction available for singles with a modified AGI of

Type of Tax-Advantaged Arrangement	Main Features	Income Limits
		$65,000–$80,000, and $130,000–$160,000 for joint filers.
Higher-education tax credits	HOPE credit: up to $1,500 per student for first and second year of post-secondary education Lifetime Learning credit: per household—$1,000 for 2001 and 2002; $2,000 after 2002	Phases out between a modified AGI of $40,000–$50,000 for singles; $80,000–$100,000 for joint filers
IRA distributions for higher-education expenses	Taxable to same extent as other IRA distributions, but exempt from 10 percent premature distribution penalty	None
Education-assistance plan	Up to $5,250 of employer-provided education assistance is tax-free Does not have to be job-related education After 2001, includes graduate study	None

CHAPTER

6

Estate Planning
Ideas

The 2001 Tax Act's repeal of the federal "death" tax turns out to provide less relief from estate planning chores than most people expected. As detailed below as well as in Chapter 1, the federal estate tax phases down starting in 2002 until it is completely repealed in 2010. Amounts exempt from estate tax will increase during the transition period, and the maximum rate of tax on estates and gifts will decrease. The gift tax phases down, too, but is not repealed completely.

Accompanying those advantages in 2010, however, will be some generally unfavorable changes to the income tax rules for inherited property, especially for those with large estates. During the phase-down period, when the exempted amount reaches $3.5 million (in 2009), complications with preexisting estate plans could arise that could cause a surviving spouse to receive no property outright. Still, proper planning during this period may result in large tax savings for some. Another change may cause some states to add or increase their own death taxes, since they will be losing revenue as a result of the repeal of the state death tax credit. Then in 2011, the repeal of the estate tax will "sunset," returning all of the estate and gift tax rules back to where they would have been had there been no repeal.

As was previously the case, estate and gift planning strategies can still protect significant amounts of property from being subject to transfer taxes. However, there is less certainty now as to what the best solutions will be. This chapter focuses on planning ideas to consider.

How the Estate and Gift Tax Works

Estate and gift taxes currently work in tandem as a "unified" transfer tax system, with basically the same tax rates and exemption amounts applying to both taxes. It's sort of "pay me now or pay me later." But as the amount exempt from estate tax increases above $1 million in the future, and the estate tax is eventually repealed, the gift tax exemption amount will be frozen at the $1 million level. Also, the gift tax will continue, although at a reduced rate, during 2010 when the estate tax is scheduled to be repealed.

Observation: Even if you have fully used your gift tax exemption of $675,000, you will be able to make tax-free gifts of up to $325,000 in 2002 (this is in addition to your annual exclusion).

Amounts Exempt from Tax

You may transfer $10,000 ($20,000 for most married couples) each year to each of an unlimited number of individuals free of gift tax. This figure will be increased for inflation. It is $11,000 ($22,000 for married couples) in 2002. To qualify for this annual exclusion, the recipient generally must have immediate access to the gift, although some gifts in trust can qualify, as can contributions to a qualified tuition program. Unlimited amounts can be transferred directly to an educational institution or health care provider free of gift tax to pay someone else's tuition or medical expenses.

But there are even bigger breaks. You can transfer unlimited amounts to your spouse free of gift or estate tax. In addition, in 2001 (it goes up in future years), you are able to transfer $675,000 to children and others without paying any estate or gift tax. This special exemption covers gifts made during life and transfers at death. Even better, annual exclusion, tuition, medical, and spousal transfers don't count against the exemption. (Special rules may apply, however, if your spouse is not a U.S. citizen.)

A special deduction combined with the $675,000 exemption amount now permits qualified family-owned business interests to shelter from gift and estate taxes as much as $1.3 million.

The 2001 Tax Act raises the $675,000 exemption amount to $3.5 million in 2009, as shown in the following table.

Estate and Gift Tax Exemption Allowances

Year	Estate Tax Exemption	Gift Tax Exemption
2001	$675,000	$675,000
2002	$1 million	$1 million
2003	$1 million	$1 million
2004	$1.5 million	$1 million
2005	$1.5 million	$1 million
2006	$2 million	$1 million
2007	$2 million	$1 million
2008	$2 million	$1 million
2009	$3.5 million	$1 million
2010	N/A (tax repealed)	$1 million
2011 and later	$1 million	$1 million

Starting in 2004, when the estate tax exemption increases to $1.5 million, the special deduction for qualified family owned business interests, mentioned above, will be repealed.

Gift and Estate Tax Rates

After you have exceeded the exemption amount, the following estate and gift tax rates apply for 2001:

For Taxable Gifts and Estates Above	Rate
$675,000	37%
$750,000	39%
$1,000,000	41%
$1,250,000	43%
$1,500,000	45%
$2,000,000	49%
$2,500,000	53%
$3,000,000	55%

The benefit of the graduated rates phases out for very large estates, effectively increasing the top rate to 60 percent for taxable estate assets between $10 million and about $17 million.

Starting in 2002, the 2001 Tax Act eliminates this 60 percent rate on these large estates. The 2001 Tax Act also will reduce the maximum estate and gift tax rates as follows:

Year	Highest Estate and Gift Tax Rates
2001	55%
2002	50%
2003	49%
2004	48%
2005	47%
2006	46%
2007	45%
2008	45%
2009	45%
2010	35% (gift tax) 0% (estate tax)
2011 and later	55%

Estate tax rates may be even higher than you think because lifetime taxable gifts are added to property owned at death for purposes of computing the estate tax rate, although your estate will receive a credit for gift taxes paid on the lifetime taxable gifts.

Currently, the recipient of most property transferred at death receives a basis equal to the fair market value of the property as of the date of death. This means that income tax is avoided on the increase in the value of the property that occurred during the decedent's life, and the recipient can sell the asset immediately and not pay any capital gains tax.

The rule is different for gifts made during life. Here, the recipient gets your basis, so if he or she sells the gift property after receipt, he or she pays capital gains tax on any appreciation that has occurred since you acquired it. On the plus side, the recipient gets to include your holding period in determining whether a sale by him or her qualifies for favorable long-term capital gains treatment.

With capital gains rates as low as 20 percent—and even lower for children and grandchildren who are in the 15 percent income tax bracket—it still may be worth considering whether lifetime giving makes sense in spite of the lack of basis step-up for lifetime gifts. Be sure to consider both the income tax and the transfer tax consequences.

In 2010, when the estate tax is due to be repealed, the basis step-up (basis is increased to the property's value at the time of transfer) for assets received from a decedent will be limited. Inheritors of property from decedents dying in 2010 will receive a basis step-up that will eliminate capital gains tax on a total of no more than $1.3 million of gain that occurred during the decedent's life. Property inherited by a surviving spouse will get an additional $3 million of basis increase, allowing a total basis increase of up to $4.3 million.

Observation: The basis step-up limit change will not affect smaller estates. However, it will add income tax complications to estate planning considerations for those with larger estates.

Observation: Only property transferred outright to the surviving spouse or held in a special form of trust known as a QTIP (Qualified Terminable Interest Property) trust qualifies for the additional $3 million of basis increase for property passing to surviving spouses. Many persons have estate plans in which bequests to surviving spouses are held in other forms of trusts that qualify for the marital deduction for estate tax purposes, but not for purposes of the $3 million basis increase—for example, general power of appointment trusts or estate trusts. Although such estate planning may be adequate if death occurs before 2010, these trusts may not be sufficient if death occurs in 2010, because the opportunity to step up the basis an additional $3 million may be lost.

Observation: In the past, estate plans often provided that retirement assets or other assets that may not be stepped up be left to the surviving spouse rather than children or other heirs. Under the new law, the reverse may be desirable, since it may be necessary to use the maximum amount of step-up for post-2009 transfers to a surviving spouse. It is important to consider income tax consequences other than the step-up, such as the option to make certain IRA withdrawal elections that are limited only to the surviving spouse.

An estate's executor will choose which of a decedent's assets will receive the basis increase. Donors and executors will also be required to report information about certain transfers, including basis and holding period information, to the IRS and to donees and estate beneficiaries.

Observation: If some beneficiaries receive higher-basis property, other beneficiaries may be burdened with higher capital gains on the sale of the property they inherit. Planning will be needed to make the most of available basis step-up and to keep potential for family strife over this issue to a minimum.

Observation: For those interested in leaving assets to charity, retirement assets remain an excellent choice because retirement assets do not qualify for a step-up in basis either before or after the repeal of the estate tax.

Planning for Phase-down and Repeal of the Estate Tax

What will all of these changes mean for you? They will mean more, rather than less, estate planning.

First, you will have to be sure that during the transition period from now through 2009, when exemption amounts are increasing and maximum tax rates are dropping, your existing will and your overall estate plan still do what you intended. If not, you will have to make adjustments.

Second, you will need to stay on top of future changes to the estate and gift tax rules. Most estate planning experts doubt that the new rules will be implemented as they are now written. As for complete repeal of the estate tax—even for one year—most say not to count on it. But no one's crystal ball can predict how the political or economic climate will change over the next decade. Only time will tell.

Planning will be easiest for those with relatively modest estates. For them, the increases in the exemption amounts through 2009 could eliminate all estate tax liability. Many will not need more than simple wills, without even the usual credit shelter trusts, to avoid estate taxes. However, if their estates increase in size or the estate tax returns to its 2001 state after 2010, that won't be true. New, more complicated plans will again be necessary.

During the phase-out period, flexibility will be needed. Some planners have suggested increasing the use of disclaimers (an election to decline the receipt of inherited property) to give surviving spouses the ability to balance estate tax savings with other financial needs. Wills may benefit from contingency language that would cause alternative provisions to kick in if the expected estate tax changes, repeal, and/or reinstatement do not occur as scheduled.

As has been the case previously, there are many tax-saving ideas you can use to reduce your estate. They are particularly helpful to higher-net-worth individuals. One quick way to figure out whether you need estate tax planning is to look at your net worth (what you own less what you owe) and add the face value of the life insurance you own. If the total exceeds the exemption amount, think about some or all of these planning ideas.

The sooner you act, the better. That's because a gift made now removes future appreciation from your estate.

Example: Take the case of an individual who used his exemption to make a $600,000 gift in 1987, when that was the maximum exemption amount. He died in 2001 when the gift's value had grown to almost $2.3 million (assuming it grew at a 10 percent annual rate). Thus, he effectively removed almost $2.3 million from his estate by acting early. In addition, the first $75,000 of his estate is sheltered by his remaining exemption allowance ($675,000 allowance for 2001 less $600,000 used in 1987). Had he not made the gift, his estate would have been increased by almost $1.7 million.

 Observation: Those with large estates should consider maximizing the early-giving strategy beginning in 2002, when the gift tax exclusion amount increases to $1 million.

Draft a Will

Many people do not have a will. As a result, their state of residence generally will determine who receives their property at death and how and when the property is received. If you are married with children, in most states your surviving spouse will not receive all your assets. In addition, you will miss the opportunity to generate some significant estate tax savings for your family.

Even if your estate is less than the estate and gift tax exemption allowance, you need a will to name a guardian for your minor children.

Review How Your Property Is Owned

Unless you live in a community property state (Arizona, California, Idaho, Louisiana, Nevada, New Mexico, Texas, Washington, Wisconsin, and, under certain circumstances, Alaska), in which all property acquired during marriage is treated as half-owned by each spouse, it is important for a married couple to consider how their property is owned.

For married couples, joint ownership with right of survivorship can be the ruin of an otherwise excellent estate plan, because the surviving spouse will automatically receive the property at the death of the first spouse. You may want it to go to your children or someone else. Although no estate tax will be paid because of the unlimited spousal allowance under the existing law, there might not be enough property to fund other estate planning options, such as the credit shelter or family trust (see page 197).

An asset ownership review can also help determine whether gifts or property transfers should occur during life between spouses to make sure that each spouse has sufficient property in his or her name alone to help fund a credit shelter or family trust.

 Observation: This review of your assets will be more crucial than ever as exemption amounts increase over the next eight years.

Consider State Death Taxes

The 2001 Tax Act gradually phases out and then completely repeals the state death tax credit allowable against the federal estate tax. The credit will be 75 percent of the current credit for decedents dying in 2002, 50 percent for those dying in 2003, and 25 percent for those dying in 2004. In 2005, the credit will be repealed and replaced by a deduction for those taxes actually paid to any state on a decedent's gross estate.

Observation: The state death tax credit is an important source of revenue for many states. It is anticipated that some state death taxes will reappear to make up for repeal of the credit. This may influence the state you choose to live in for retirement.

Observation: Many formula bequests under existing wills factor in the state death tax credit. Estate plans should be examined to make sure that intended results are not changed by this tax law revision.

Give Gifts

Over time, a gift giving program can remove hundreds of thousands of dollars from your estate on a tax-free basis. You can give up to $10,000 ($20,000 if your spouse joins in the gift) to each of any number of people each year, and you will not have to pay gift tax. These figures are increased for inflation, and will be $11,000 ($22,000 for couples) in 2002. Making these "annual exclusion" gifts removes property from your estate at no gift or estate tax cost, often shifting income-earning property to family members in lower income tax brackets. You also remove future appreciation in the value of the gift from your estate.

In addition, there is an unlimited exclusion for tuition you paid directly to a school or medical care payments you made directly to a health care provider on someone else's behalf. These tuition and medical payments are gift tax-free, and they don't count toward the $10,000 ($11,000 in 2002) annual gift tax exclusion. Thus, a grandparent can pay tuition directly to a school on behalf of a grandchild, pay the orthodontist for the grandchild's braces, and give the grandchild $10,000 per year ($11,000 in 2002) without using up any lifetime allowance.

Observation: Tuition payments for a private elementary school, secondary school, or college all qualify, as long as a contribution to the school would generate a charitable contribution deduction. Room and board, books, and similar expenses do not qualify for the exclusion.

It should be noted that payments by parents and grandparents to a qualified state tuition program don't qualify for the unlimited tuition gift tax break. Payments by parents and grandparents to these tax-favored college savings programs do count toward the tax-free annual limit. However, you can choose to treat a contribution for a beneficiary that's over $10,000 ($11,000 in 2002) as made equally over five years. Thus, a $50,000 ($55,000 in 2002) gift to a state tuition program for a single beneficiary in a single year can be gift tax free. For the next four years, though, you couldn't give the beneficiary any additional annual exclusion gifts.

 Observation: Do not wait until late in the year to make gifts. Instead, make them in January each year. In a good year, an asset that's worth $10,000 in January could be worth significantly more in December. By giving early, the postgift appreciation also escapes gift tax.

Valuation Discounts

Transfers of certain types of assets, typically a minority interest in a business enterprise, may permit the use of a valuation discount for gift and estate tax purposes (so that the value for these purposes is below market value). The value of the underlying property does not change, but how the property is owned may generate discounts.

Example: The true fair market value of Asset A is $100. Asset A, for valid business reasons, is placed into a vehicle that is friendly to valuation discounts, such as a limited partnership. When all the limited partnership interests are given to children, the value reported on the gift tax return might be only $70, a 30 percent discount from the underlying fair market value because of the minority interest and lack of marketability. Limited partnership and limited liability companies offer many nontax advantages, including retention of control and some protection from creditors of the donee.

Observation: The IRS has challenged valuation discounts taken when family limited partnership interests are given away in "deathbed" transfers—those very close to the individual's death. Also, you must disclose claimed valuation discounts on your gift tax return.

If you own a majority interest in a business, you can make gifts of nonvoting shares or small amounts of voting shares which would be entitled to a minority discount that would be unavailable if they passed at your death. Such gifts would not receive a basis step-up at your death, but future appreciation would be out of your estate. If your lifetime gifts of voting shares brought your voting rights below 50 percent, all of your shares would be entitled to a minority discount at your death.

 Caution: If you own a limited partnership, limited liability company, or non-voting shares while still controlling the entity, you will not get a minority discount on any of the interests you own.

Consider Trusts

Credit Shelter or Family Trust

Married couples should now have at least this one basic trust if their combined assets exceed the estate and gift tax exemption allowance amount. Failure to have this trust can cost your family hundreds of thousands of dollars in estate taxes that could have been avoided.

Fully funded credit shelter trusts will still be needed by spouses with very large estates. However, the increases in estate tax exemptions will require those with relatively modest estates to reexamine the impact of credit shelter trusts. These provisions ensure that both spouses' estates get the full estate tax exemption. Their purpose is to leave trusts for children or other heirs with the maximum that can pass to them without estate tax, and to give surviving spouses only a limited interest in that portion of a decedent's estate. These provisions were designed around exemption amounts ranging from $675,000 to $1 million (to which the exempt amount previously was scheduled to rise in 2006). As the exemption increases under the 2001 Tax Act, however, these arrangements will be funded with larger and larger amounts—and possibly all—of a decedent's assets, in some cases leaving nothing outright to the surviving spouse. If the surviving spouse has sufficient assets of other kinds, and maximizing estate tax savings is the prime consideration, that may be desirable. But in other situations use of the credit shelter trust could cause serious financial problems for the surviving spouse.

Observation: Many wills now automatically increase the credit shelter's funding as the exemption amount rises. You can avoid this by specifying in your will the maximum amount of your estate that should fund a credit shelter trust.

Life Insurance Trust

If you have a life insurance policy, consider giving the policy to a life insurance trust or having the trust purchase a new policy directly from the life insurance company. The policy proceeds can escape estate tax.

Observation: Life insurance needs for estate liquidity may decrease as the estate tax is phased out and repealed, but the need will not be eliminated because of the loss of full basis step-up and the possibility of reinstatement of the estate tax in 2011. You will have to take a variety of contingencies into account in drafting and funding a life insurance trust, particularly the anticipated need for quick access to cash.

Grantor Retained Annuity Trust

Sometimes referred to as the "have your cake and eat it, too" trust, this trust is popular because it permits you to give away future appreciation on property placed into the trust while retaining the property's value. You even receive an IRS-determined benchmark rate of return on the value. If the trust assets provide a rate of return over the IRS benchmark rate of return, the trust's beneficiaries will receive the excess (either in further trust or outright) at a very low gift tax cost.

Typical assets placed in this type of trust include S corporation stock, publicly traded stock, and other assets expected to give a rate of return of over about 8 percent annually. The higher the rate of return, the more assets will go to the trust's beneficiaries.

Observation: Gifts to these trusts are particularly attractive in periods of low interest rates because it should be easier to exceed the IRS benchmark rate of return. (This interest rate varies from month to month based on interest rates on U.S. Treasury Securities.)

Qualified Personal Residence Trust

You can transfer a personal residence (either a first or second home) to the beneficiaries of a qualified personal residence trust at a discount from the home's current fair market value. You can live in the home for the term of the trust and continue to take a mortgage interest deduction as well as a real estate tax deduction. When your interest in the trust ends, you can rent the home from the trust beneficiaries at fair market value rates (an excellent means of further reducing your estate).

A qualified personal residence trust is especially desirable if significant appreciation is expected in the value of the home over time, because the appreciation that occurs after the trust is established can also escape estate and gift taxation (see also page 146).

Observation: Unlike grantor retained annuity trusts, gifts to these trusts are less attractive in periods of low interest rates because the gift tax cost is higher than it would be in periods of higher interest rates.

Dynasty Trust

A dynasty trust allows you to provide for your descendants (usually your grandchildren and more remote descendants) without gift, estate, or generation-skipping transfer tax consequences to your descendants. Such trusts are typically designed to last for the longest possible period allowed by law. Typically, the trustee (the individual or entity that manages the trust assets and income) will have the discretion to pay trust income and principal to your descendants. The trusts are intended to take advantage of some part or the entire amount that you can transfer to your grandchildren or more remote descendants without incurring the generation-skipping transfer tax. This amount is $1 million (as indexed for inflation) for 2001 through 2003; for 2004 through 2009, it will equal the estate tax exemption amount as shown on the chart on page 184. A dynasty trust can be established during life or in a will.

Charitable Remainder Trust

If you are concerned because you have built up an asset base that is not producing sufficient cash flow for you, this trust may help. The rate of return is flexible—the cash-flow yield can be improved to 5 percent or higher on the value of your asset base. At the end of the term of the trust, the remaining trust principal will pass to charity. Because these trusts are tax-exempt entities, they generally don't pay income tax upon the sale of any low-basis assets used to fund the trust.

Observation: You can use some of the extra cash flow that you receive from this asset transfer and establish a life insurance trust for your family to replace the assets placed in the charitable remainder trust, which go to charity at your death. However, life insurance is not a required adjunct to a charitable remainder trust.

Intentionally Defective Trust

Transfers into this kind of trust are gifts, but the person making the gift is still liable for the tax on income earned by the trust. The benefit? The payment of the income tax provides an indirect advantage to the trust beneficiaries, yet it's not considered a further gift to them. The "defective" aspect refers to the fact that the person setting up the trust is liable for income taxes. Normally, that's bad. But for high-networth individuals, a defective trust can save a family a significant amount of estate taxes. Further tax savings may be obtained by selling property to the trust for a promissory note. If properly structured, the growth in the trust assets that exceeds the interest rate on the note may pass to your heirs free of gift or estate taxes.

Qualified Domestic Trust

A QDOT is a special trust that qualifies for the estate tax marital deduction if the surviving spouse is not a U.S. citizen. Generally, the estate tax is deferred until the death of the surviving spouse, at which time an estate tax must be paid based on the value of the trust principal remaining. If distributions of trust principal are paid out to the surviving spouse before death, estate tax is also generally payable based on the value of that distribution. Under the 2001 Tax Act, the QDOT principal will escape estate taxation at death if the surviving spouse dies in 2010 or thereafter. Also, any distributions of principal from a QDOT to a living spouse would remain subject to the estate tax through 2020 but would be free of estate tax in 2021. (Because 2021 occurs after the December 31, 2010, sunset date, this latter provision is in effect nullified by the Act.)

Observation: It is possible to avoid completely estate tax for a QDOT established before 2010 where the surviving spouse dies in 2010 or thereafter. QDOTs, therefore, should be considered for use in the estate plan of any person married to a non–U.S. citizen.

Stock Option Trust

Consider putting your nonqualified stock options in trust for your children. Although you must pay income tax on the value of the options when they are exercised, you may save your children a big estate and gift tax bite. Most option plans must be amended to allow this type of transfer.

Give a Roth IRA

Fund a Roth IRA for 2001 and 2002 if the recipient has at least $2,000 of earned income each year and doesn't exceed the income limitation (see Chapter 3).

 Observation: Gifts of IRA contributions are an excellent way for parents and grandparents to help their children and grandchildren accumulate significant retirement assets.

Pay Gift Taxes Now

Under a peculiar quirk in the Tax Code, it can be less costly to prepay gift taxes than to pay estate taxes after death. Individuals with large estates might consider making large gifts and paying significant gift taxes prior to death. One must survive at least three years after the payment of a gift tax to realize the savings. Not only will future appreciation escape estate tax, but a lower overall transfer tax can result. With the prospect of estate tax repeal in 2010, however, the idea of paying any substantial amount of gift tax now becomes much less appealing. Very old or unhealthy taxpayers who may live more than three years are the most likely candidates for this strategy.

Idea Checklist

☐ Review your will and estate plan to determine what adjustments are needed to benefit from the 2001 Tax Act changes to the estate and gift tax and to avoid potentially costly pitfalls. Especially consider whether you need to change or eliminate an existing credit shelter trust arrangement.

☐ Use asset ownership forms that maximize estate tax savings (such as limited liability companies or limited partnerships).

☐ Review the use of joint ownership.

☐ Make $10,000 gifts each year ($11,000 for 2002).

☐ Pay tuition expenses directly to an educational institution or make a payment to a health care provider. Consider a multiyear tuition gift, where appropriate.

☐ Move life insurance into a life insurance trust.

☐ Put rapidly appreciating assets into a grantor retained annuity trust or sell them to an intentionally defective trust.

☐ Set things up to take advantage of any available valuation discounts.

The bottom line is that Congress has opened a window of opportunity for taxpayers to optimize their estate and gift planning. It is important to take advantage of these opportunities as soon as possible.

YEAR-END
TAX SAVING
STRATEGIES

Quick Planning Guide

Despite the best intentions, George W. Bush's tax-cutting coup was inevitably beset by all the legalistic delays, distinctions, and exceptions that often turn vibrant new laws into meek promissory notes.

In fact, the 2001 Tax Act provides many new tax breaks, including a small cut for 2001, for which taxpayers don't have to do a thing. But most of the new tax savers don't kick in until 2002. So it is still a good idea to reduce taxes as much as possible for 2001 and 2002 with tried-and-true year-end strategies. Though this will require a little advance planning, it will be worth the effort.

What are the best year-end tax-planning strategies? They are those that produce the largest overall tax savings, taking both 2001 and 2002 into account. There are three basic techniques:

- Tax reduction
- Tax deferral
- Income shifting

Tax Reduction

Tax reduction occurs when you take action that results in payment of less tax than would otherwise have been due. For example, if you switch funds from a taxable investment (like shares of stock in a public company) to a municipal bond that earns tax-free interest, you will reduce your tax bill. Or you may want to consider contributing to a Roth IRA that can generate tax-free income instead of putting the money into a taxable investment vehicle. Another option is to shift funds from an investment such as a money-market account or CD, which produces ordinary income, to a stock fund in hopes of earning some lower-taxed long-term capital gain.

 Caution: When doing your tax planning, don't forget about investment fundamentals. You want to find a prudent investment balance between risk and reward, taking into account your age, your family situation, and other factors. Taxes are important, but they're far from your only consideration. Work taxes into your overall financial plan, but don't let them be the driving force behind your decision making.

Tax Deferral

Tax deferral is achieved when you earn income now and pay tax on it in the future. Your retirement plan is an example. Although your retirement investments generate income throughout the years, they are generally taxed only when you receive them.

Deferring the receipt of taxable income can save you money, even if it produces little or no tax savings, because you can use your money longer before paying the IRS. That means greater compounding of earnings for you. On the other hand, accelerating income, even if you think you will be in a higher tax bracket in later years, means you will pay the IRS sooner than otherwise might be required. Loss of the use of that money cuts down on the advantage you hoped to attain.

Another deferral technique is to move up deductions from a later year to an earlier year so that you get the benefit of them sooner. But don't "overaccelerate" deduction items to defer taxes. Remember that in order to get the deduction sooner, you usually have to lay out the dollars sooner, which means you lose the use of those dollars. For example, an individual in the 39.1 percent tax bracket for 2001 who accelerates a $5,000 deduction into 2001 defers $1,955 of tax. This may make economic sense if the deduction is shifted from January to December, but it is not beneficial for long periods of time because the funds you had to shell out to generate the deduction would lose more investment income in five months than the amount you gain from accelerating the tax deduction at 39.1 percent for one year. If you are in the 15 percent bracket, you generally should not accelerate any deductions that could be paid later than February. Further care should be taken; not all expenses can be accelerated without limit. Also, moving up certain deductions, such as state income taxes, could trigger the Alternative Minimum Tax (AMT) (see Chapter 10).

Observation: Sometimes a single move (see "Income Shifting," below) can combine tax reduction and tax deferral. Tax rates above the 15 percent bracket will be dropping again in 2002. So if you can shift ordinary income from 2001 to 2002, you will not only defer your tax liability, but also owe tax at a lower rate (assuming that your financial circumstances are about the same from year to year).

Income Shifting

Income shifting generally involves transferring income-producing property to someone who is taxed at a lower rate. One example is giving dividend-paying stock to a lower-taxed family member. For example, you may have stock in a mature company that isn't growing much but pays a healthy dividend. If you're in the 35.5 percent tax bracket for 2001, you will pay $355 in taxes on every $1,000 of dividends you receive. If you give some of the stock to a child or grandchild in the 15 percent tax bracket, tax on the dividends will be cut to $150 per $1,000.

Observation: Starting in 2002, when dependents will be able to benefit from the 10 percent bracket, the potential tax savings from shifting ordinary income such as interest and dividends will be even greater. Tax on dividends can be as little as $100 per $1,000.

Caution: The so-called kiddie tax (which taxes children's investment income at their parents' rate) keeps this family income-shifting strategy from working for children under age 14. All but a small amount of the unearned income of a child under 14 is taxed at his or her parents' top rate.

Tax saving techniques are described in Chapters 8 and 9. Before turning to these chapters, however, it is important to review how capital gains and the AMT affect your tax liability this year (see below), when year-end tax saving strategies may work very well for you.

For more details on accelerating deductions, see Chapter 8. For more on deferring income, see Chapter 9.

Year-End Capital Gains Checkup

With a few exceptions, 2001 wasn't a very good year for stock market investors. The Dow performed well at first, then took a nosedive, recovered to hit a new high, then dropped off again and meandered in a rather sorry trading range before dropping precipitously later in the year. A roller coaster comes to mind: big ups and downs at first, and then smaller ones, finishing right where you started. The NASDAQ was much worse. There, the downs were a lot worse than the ups. The Federal Reserve did its bit by cutting short-term interest rates over and over, but the sluggish economy refused to take the bait. Consumers kept spending, but corporate earnings weakened, causing corporations to cut spending. The tragic events of September 11, 2001, have had and will have significant impact on our economy and the financial markets.

Those who took profits on long-term gains near market highs will get the benefit of favorable capital gains tax rates. Investors whose gains are short-term are less fortunate. Those gains are taxed at regular income tax rates.

If you are among the majority of investors with recent losses, you may be able to get some tax advantages from them. You can offset capital gains—even short-term gains—and up to an additional $3,000 of other income with your losses.

For example, suppose you have a $10,000 gain on some stock in a company that has done well over the years, but which you think is due for a fall. If you sell some other stock at a $10,000 loss, you will be able to sell your gain stock and fully offset your tax liability with your loss. If you recognized a total of $13,000 of losses during the year, you could offset your $10,000 capital gain and use the extra $3,000 loss to offset $3,000 of other income, such as interest, dividends, or compensation income. If your excess losses come to more than $3,000, you have to carry them over to future years, when they can offset capital gains and up to $3,000 of ordinary income (for more details about capital gains and losses, see Chapter 2).

You have a great deal of flexibility at year-end to control the timing of investment decisions in order to maximize your tax savings. As year-end approaches, review your investment results. Calculate gains and losses and compare them with unrealized gains or losses you currently hold. (See Chapter 2 for more information on netting capital gains and losses.) As we said before, in making these tax decisions, you must also consider your individual financial and personal situation and the economic viability of particular investments. Taxes are but one factor to consider. You may also want to consider the impact of further reduced capital gains rates for five-year gains that are available beginning in 2001.

Year-End Alternative Minimum Tax Diagnosis

The AMT is a separate tax system under which certain types of items receive different—usually less favorable—tax treatment than under the regular income tax system. For example, state and local income taxes and real estate taxes are deductible under the regular system but are not deductible by you under the AMT. And the standard deduction, personal exemptions, some medical expenses, interest on home-equity loans, and miscellaneous itemized deductions, which you can claim for regular tax purposes, don't reduce your AMT. Also, the bargain element on incentive stock options (ISOs) that you exercise (the difference between the exercise price and the stock's value at exercise) isn't subject to regular income tax in the year of exercise but is subject to the AMT. You must calculate taxes under both systems and pay the higher tax bill. (For a more detailed explanation of the AMT, see Chapter 10.)

Planning for the AMT can be difficult because many factors can trigger it. If you believe that you are within range of the AMT, year-end strategies may help reduce your tax liability. If you are subject to the AMT, you may want to go a counterintuitive route and do the complete opposite of the normal year-end tax planning strategy. For example, individuals subject to the AMT might benefit from accelerating ordinary income items into 2001 and deferring until 2002 deductions that are not allowed for AMT purposes, such as state and local taxes and miscellaneous itemized deductions.

If your 2001 year includes any of the items in the following list, you may need tax planning to avoid the AMT:

- Exercise of incentive stock options (as opposed to nonqualified stock options) for which the stock is held past December 31, 2001.
- Large prior-year state or local tax balance due, paid in April 2001.
- Large fourth-quarter state or local estimated tax payment made in January 2001, rather than in December 2000.
- Expenses that exceed 2 percent of income for investment management or tax planning services or unreimbursed employee business expenses.
- Tax-exempt municipal bond income from "private activity bonds."
- Business interests owned in S corporation or partnership form, in which these entities own significant amounts of depreciable assets.
- Large long-term capital gains.
- Interest on home-equity debt that is deductible for regular income tax purposes.
- Passive activity losses that are allowable for regular tax purposes.

Now that the three basic tax planning strategies have been reviewed, this study will move on to more sophisticated techniques, starting with accelerating deductions, which is the subject of our next chapter.

Accelerating Deductions

A great tax deduction is like a great golf swing: use it or lose it. Moreover, use it right now—deductions don't appreciate. The sooner they're claimed, the better they work.

Accelerating deductions into an earlier year gives taxpayers their benefits sooner. Also, because of the scheduled 2001 Tax Act rate cut for 2002, deductions that are moved up into 2001 are more valuable because they will be used to lower your income for 2001, when the tax rates are higher—so you'll pay less tax.

Obviously, the goal is to use deductions to their full potential, keeping in mind that itemized deductions provide a tax benefit only if their total is more than the standard deduction amount.

Example: The standard deduction for a married couple filing a joint return for 2001 is $7,600. If you accelerate deductions from 2002 into 2001 and it turns out that your 2001 itemized deductions total less than $7,600, your effort hasn't increased the amount of deductions you can claim in 2001. In addition, you have lost the opportunity to take that accelerated deduction in 2002.

Equally important is something everyone knows but few act on—keep track of your deductions as they occur, not six or seven months later. If nothing is more painful than trying to reconstruct credible expenses that are barely remembered, then nothing is easier than keeping expense records current and ready for a running start on accelerated deductions.

If you determine that it pays to itemize deductions for the current year (based on the figures listed below), there are certain steps you can take to move up deductible expenses. As a general rule, you should pay deductible bills and expenses received this year, rather than waiting until next year to pay them.

If you want to move up deductions into this year, you can mail a check for a deductible item postmarked as late as December 31 and still claim it on this year's return, even though the check won't be cashed until next year. In the same way, deductible items charged on a credit card by year-end can generally be deducted on the current year's return, even if the credit card bill is not paid until the following year.

If your itemized deductions come close to the standard deduction amount each year (for 2001 the standard deduction is $7,600 for joint returns and

$4,550 for singles), you can benefit by "bunching" itemized expenses in alternative years so that you can itemize every other year. Bunching strategies include planning larger charitable gifts, making January mortgage payments in December, accelerating or delaying real estate taxes and state and local income tax payments, and timing elective surgery and other medical expenses prior to year-end (though keeping in mind that cosmetic surgery is not deductible).

 Observation: Deduction bunching works best for those who don't have recurring deductible expenses every year in excess of the standard deduction amount. For example, if you pay mortgage interest and state and local taxes each year that are more than your standard deduction amount, bunching won't help you. But if you have itemized deductions each year that are close to, but under, the standard deduction amount, bunching could work well for you. You might be able to itemize one year and claim the standard deduction the next, increasing your overall deductions and reducing your tax bills.

State and Local Taxes

State and local income taxes and real estate taxes are deductible in the year paid.

If you would benefit from accelerating deductions, consider December payments of state and local estimated taxes that are due in January. You also could move up the payment of any balance due in April to the previous year-end, but it may be more beneficial to invest those funds for the 3½-month period, particularly if your marginal tax bracket is below 28 percent.

If you have an unusually large amount of income in 2001, and will have a large balance due on your state or local return in April 2002, you should consider prepaying the amount in December 2001, so that you can "match" the state and local tax deduction with the income that generated it. This technique can help you avoid or minimize the impact of the AMT on your 2002 tax return.

 Caution: If you are subject to the Alternative Minimum Tax, you may lose any tax savings that result from the deduction of state and local taxes because the deduction is not permitted in calculating the AMT.

Interest

You can't deduct all interest paid on borrowed money. There are six different kinds of interest for tax purposes—home mortgage (see Chapter 4), business, investment, passive activity, student loan (see Chapter 5), and personal—and the deductibility of each type is treated differently. Generally, the way borrowed funds are used determines their category.

Business Interest

If you "materially participate" in the operation and management of a pass-through entity (a partnership, LLC, or S corporation) or an unincorporated business, you may generally fully deduct interest on business-related borrowings.

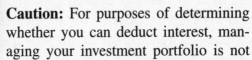

Caution: For purposes of determining whether you can deduct interest, managing your investment portfolio is not considered a business. Deductibility of investment interest is more limited, as discussed below.

Also, the IRS and most courts say that interest on a sole proprietor's business-related tax deficiency is nondeductible personal interest.

Investment Interest

Interest on money that you borrow to purchase "portfolio" investments (such as stocks, mutual funds, bonds, and the like) that produce dividends, interest, royalties, or annuity income is deductible only to the extent that the portfolio produces taxable income. You may carry forward indefinitely any excess and deduct it against your investment income in later years. To maximize your deductible investment interest, try to match investment income with investment interest expenses. Note that such interest is not deductible to the extent that the borrowing was used to purchase or carry tax-exempt municipal bonds.

You can also elect to include long-term capital gains as investment income against which investment interest may be deducted. If you make this election, however, these gains will be taxed at ordinary income rates rather than at the lower capital gains rates. The effect of the election is to save tax currently on your excess investment interest expense at a 20 percent capital gains rate. This election makes sense when you expect that you will have excess investment interest expense for the foreseeable future.

Passive Activity Interest

Your share of interest incurred or paid on a passive activity investment is in most cases deductible only up to the amount of your income from all passive activities that year. A passive activity investment is generally:

1. an investment in an operating business in which you do not "materially participate"; or
2. an investment in real estate or another "tax shelter." However, renting real estate to yourself or your business won't generate passive income. Generally, all limited partnership investments are considered passive activities.

You may carry forward any excess passive losses and use them to offset passive activity income in future years. Also, you can usually deduct suspended passive losses in the year you sell your interest in the particular investment. When there is a sale or other disposition of a passive activity in a taxable transaction, net passive losses are applied first against income or gain from other passive activities. Then, any remaining losses are reclassified as nonpassive and can offset nonpassive income such as compensation income or portfolio income, including interest and dividends.

Example: In the year you sell your ownership interest in a real estate limited partnership, you have $10,000 of passive losses left after offsetting all available passive income for the year, including any gain from the sale of the property used in the activity. On your return for that year you may deduct the $10,000 against your nonpassive income sources.

If your adjusted gross income (AGI) is under $100,000, a special exception permits you to deduct as much as $25,000 of passive rental real estate losses resulting from interest and other deductions if you actively participate in the management of the business. This exception phases out as AGI increases to $150,000.

Example: You own a beach house that you rent out for the season each year. You have an agent who handles rentals, but you set the rental terms, approve tenants, make decisions involving maintenance and repairs, and hire contractors to do the work. Your personal use of the property is a very small percentage of the rental time. In this situation, you are an active participant in the rental real estate activity.

If your AGI is $100,000 or less, you may deduct up to $25,000 of losses from the activity each year against your other nonpassive income. If your AGI is $125,000, you can deduct up to $12,500 of rental activity losses. But in any year that your AGI is $150,000 or more, you cannot deduct any of the losses against nonpassive income.

There are even more liberal rules for investments in low-income housing and for individuals and closely held corporations that meet the definition of a "real estate professional." (See IRS Publication 527, *Residential Rental Property,* for details concerning what it takes to qualify as a real estate professional.) Tougher rules apply to losses from interests in publicly traded partnerships; losses from these activities can only offset income from the activity until the interest is disposed of.

The passive activity rules are extremely complex, and if you think you may be subject to them, you should consult your tax adviser.

Student Loan Interest

There is an above-the-line deduction (these deductions are subtracted directly from your gross income to calculate AGI)—available even to individuals who do not itemize deductions—for interest paid on a qualified education loan. For 2001, you may deduct up to $2,500 for interest paid on qualified education loans during the first 60 months of the repayment period. Interest on student loans taken out before 1998 (the first year the deduction was available) is deductible as long as the 60-month repayment limit had not expired at that time. A loan and any refinancing or consolidation are generally treated as a single loan for purposes of the 60-month rule. The maximum deduction phases out for single taxpayers with an AGI between $40,000 and $55,000, and for married taxpayers filing jointly with an AGI between $60,000 and $75,000.

For 2002, the maximum deduction stays at $2,500, but the 2001 Tax Act repealed the 60-month limit (see Chapter 5 for more details). It also increased the phase-out range to $50,000–$65,000 of AGI for single taxpayers and $100,000–$130,000 for married couples filing jointly. The start of the phase-out thresholds will increase for inflation after 2002.

The elimination of the 60-month limit means that starting in 2002, the deduction will be available for interest paid on student loans each year, even if the repayment extends for more than five years.

Observation: Many student loans have repayment terms that extend well beyond five years. So the removal of the 60-month limitation will mean that interest on student loans will be deductible much more widely.

Example: You finished college with $30,000 of student loan debt, which you have arranged to repay over 10 years. Although you were a dependent of your parents while you were a student, you will no longer be claimed on their tax return. Before 2002, you would have qualified for the student loan interest deduction only for the first five years of interest payments. Thanks to the 2001 Tax Act, you will be able to deduct up to $2,500 of interest each year, subject to the income limits.

Qualifying loans generally include only debt incurred solely to pay the higher-education expenses for yourself, your spouse, or your children or grandchildren at the time the debt was incurred. Loans from relatives do not qualify. You must be the person legally responsible to repay the loan in order to be able to deduct the interest. So you can't deduct interest you pay, for example, on your child's loan. Nor can you deduct interest on a revolving credit line not earmarked specifically for higher-education expenses. You are also not eligible for the deduction in years when you are claimed as a dependent on someone else's tax return.

Personal Interest

Interest incurred on car loans, credit cards, or IRS adjustments or any other interest falling outside the other five categories is generally not deductible. If you can obtain a favorable interest rate, you should consider taking out a home-equity loan to pay off any of these debts, because the interest on a home-equity loan of up to $100,000 can be claimed as an itemized deduction, except for the purposes of the AMT (see Chapter 4).

Medical Expenses

You can deduct unreimbursed medical expenses (including those of your spouse and dependents) to the extent that they exceed 7.5 percent of your AGI (10 percent for the AMT). Doctors' and dentists' fees, hospital bills, and prescription drugs are deductible to the extent not covered by insurance. In addition, your payments for health insurance and certain long-term-care insurance and long-term-care expenses are included as medical expenses.

If medical expenses seem likely to be close to or exceed the 7.5 percent floor this year, consider accelerating elective treatment or surgery (keeping in mind that cosmetic surgery is generally not deductible as a medical expense) and paying for it before year-end. If the floor will not be reached this year but might be reached next year, consider the opposite strategy: delaying payment of medical bills whenever possible.

Other opportunities if you are self-employed include the following:

For 2001, self-employed individuals may deduct 60 percent of the annual cost of health insurance for themselves, their spouses, and their dependents. The deduction percentage is slated to increase in later years. This deduction is not allowed for months during which you are eligible to participate in an employer-provided health insurance plan (including a spouse's plan). Note that this allowance is an "adjustment to income" rather than an itemized deduction. Therefore it can be taken even by non-itemizers and is not reduced for itemizers at higher income levels.

A self-employed person also may deduct a percentage of the cost of long-term-care insurance premiums, as long as the individual is not eligible for any employer-provided long-term-care insurance (including under a spouse's plan).

The allowable deduction for self-employed medical insurance is as follows:

2001	60 percent
2002	70 percent
2003 and later	100 percent

Charitable Contributions

Charitable contributions are one of the most flexible deductible expenses, because you can usually control their timing and amount. For example, you could accelerate deductible expenses by making a contribution in December rather than January. A contribution is considered made at the time of delivery (mailing a check constitutes delivery). You cannot take a deduction based only on a pledge—you must actually make the contribution.

In general, you can deduct contributions to qualified charities of up to 50 percent of your AGI. The deductions are also allowed for AMT purposes. Any excess can be carried forward for five years.

Observation: If you plan to make charitable donations for the next few years, you should consider making them sooner while you are still in a higher tax bracket (the 2001 Tax Act will result in income being subject to lower tax rates in coming years). You can establish a donor-advised philanthropic fund as a means to get a current deduction and earn a tax-free return until you wish to donate the funds to particular charities. Donor-advised philanthropic funds can be established through community foundations as well as certain mutual fund companies and other financial and charitable organizations. The minimum contribution to establish the fund can be as low as $10,000.

Observation: Unreimbursed expenses you incur as a volunteer, including mileage driven in your car, are deductible. The mileage rate for purposes of the charitable deduction is 14 cents per mile.

Property donations

Special rules apply to donations of property to charities. If you donate appreciated property, such as securities or land, your deduction is based on the property's current market value rather than on its original cost. Contributions of appreciated capital gains property, however, are limited to 30 percent of

AGI unless a special election is made to reduce the deductible amount of the contribution.

Instead of selling property that has been held for longer than one year and has appreciated in value and then donating the proceeds, consider donating the property itself. If you sold the property and donated the proceeds, you would pay capital gains tax on any appreciation, while receiving a deduction for only the amount of cash that's left to contribute to the charity. If you donate appreciated property directly to a charity, you escape the capital gains tax and receive a deduction for the property's full fair market value.

If property that you are considering donating to charity has decreased in value, you should sell it and donate the proceeds. In addition to the charitable deduction, the sale will generate a capital loss that can be used to offset other capital gains and up to $3,000 of other income.

For contributions of appreciated property to a private foundation, the restriction that used to limit the charitable deduction for gifts of publicly traded stock to your basis in the stock no longer applies. A full fair market value deduction for contributions of "qualified appreciated stock" is permitted. Such stock must be a long-term capital asset traded on an established securities market. No more than 10 percent of the value of all of a company's outstanding stock may be contributed.

Observation: The deduction for contributions of long-term capital gains property to a private foundation is generally limited to 20 percent of AGI for any year. Any excess can be carried forward and deducted for five years.

Any charitable contribution of property other than marketable securities valued in excess of $5,000 ($10,000 for gifts of closely held stock) must be supported by a qualified appraisal completed by the extended due date of your tax return. The appraiser and a representative of the charitable organization must sign Form 8283 or the deduction will be denied. Additional requirements apply to contributions of art if a deduction of $20,000 or more is claimed.

Substantiation Requirements

The general substantiation requirements for a deductible charitable contribution are as follows:

- *Cash contributions under $250.* A canceled check is acceptable as long as no goods or services are received in exchange.
- *Cash contributions of $250 or more.* These contributions must be acknowledged in writing by the charity. You must obtain this documentation from the charity by the date your tax return is filed or the due date of the return (including any extensions), whichever is earlier. The acknowledgment must state whether the charity provided any goods or services

in return for the contribution and, if so, provide the information required for quid pro quo contributions (see below).

Observation: This rule applies only if $250 or more is given at one time. For example, if over the course of a year you make several contributions of $200 to the same charity, the substantiation requirement does not apply.

- *Noncash contributions under $250.* The donor should retain a detailed list of the items contributed, including the estimated value of the goods.
- *Noncash contributions of $250 or more.* The donor must obtain a receipt that describes the donated property (and indicates any goods or services received in exchange). The charity is not required to place a value on the property. For noncash contributions over $500, additional information must be included with the donor's tax return.

Caution: The IRS has instructed its examiners to look closely at donations of used autos. It is wise to donate only to reputable charities and to not be aggressive in valuing your donated auto. Be sure to keep evidence of its condition, such as photos and maintenance records and receipts.

- *"Quid pro quo" contributions over $75.* A quid pro quo contribution is one that is partly a charitable contribution and partly a payment for goods or services. The charity must provide the donor with a written statement that includes a good-faith estimate of the value of the goods or services provided and informs the donor that the contribution deduction is limited to the payment in excess of the value of the goods or services. Contributions are fully deductible if goods or services received from the charity are only of nominal value or when only an intangible religious benefit is received.

Deferred Giving

The most common form of charitable contribution is the "current gift," for which you transfer control of money or property to a charity and you keep no control over it.

In recent years, however, "deferred giving" has become increasingly popular. This involves an irrevocable transfer to a charity whose ultimate use of the property is deferred to some time in the future. For many, deferred gifts provide the best of all worlds: a current charitable deduction, a retained income stream, a charitable contribution to a favorite organization, and a reduction in the donor's taxable estate.

If you make substantial charitable contributions each year, consider establishing a charitable lead trust or charitable remainder trust.

In a charitable lead trust, you donate property to a trust that guarantees to pay the charity a fixed amount or a fixed percentage of the fair market value of the trust's assets for a certain number of years. At the end of the term, remaining trust assets revert to you or to a designated beneficiary, such as a child or grandchild.

In a charitable remainder trust, you transfer property to a trust, and the trust guarantees to pay you or a designated noncharitable beneficiary a fixed amount or a fixed percentage of the fair market value of the trust's assets (figured annually) for life or a term of years. At the end of the term, the remaining assets are transferred to a charity.

 Observation: The rules for establishing these charitable giving vehicles are complex. If you are planning to make a large gift, contact your tax adviser to discuss how they work.

Caution: Deductions are not allowed for transfers to charitable organizations involving the use of split-dollar life insurance arrangements if the charity pays any premium for the donor. Employers often use split-dollar life insurance arrangements to provide a substantial amount of insurance coverage for key executives or employees. Split-dollar life insurance is permanent insurance purchased under an arrangement in which the company and the individual share the cost of the policy as well as its benefits and proceeds.

Casualty Losses

If you have experienced a natural disaster or another casualty and suffer property damage, a casualty loss deduction is available to help lessen the blow of any unreimbursed losses (casualty losses are deductible to the extent that they exceed $100 beyond insurance reimbursement). In general, the amount of the loss is the lesser of the decrease in fair market value of the property or your adjusted basis (generally, your cost less depreciation deductions) in the property. Insurance reimbursements reduce the amount of the loss. In addition, the first $100 of each loss is nondeductible. However, if several items are damaged or lost in the course of a single casualty, the $100 floor is applied only once. Finally, only total allowable losses in excess of 10 percent of the AGI may be deducted.

Example: Your home was severely damaged by a lightning strike, and your loss, after insurance reimbursement, is $20,000. The first $100 of the loss is not deductible. If your AGI is $70,000, $7,000 of the remaining $19,900 loss also is nondeductible. Thus, your casualty loss deduction would be $12,900 ($19,900 minus $7,000).

If your loss occurs due to a presidentially declared disaster, such as an earthquake or hurricane, you can claim the loss either on your tax return for the year in which it occurred or on the prior year's return.

 Observation: Claiming the loss on the earlier year's return (by filing an amended return, if necessary) may get you a refund faster, but you should do the calculations both ways to see which choice results in the largest tax savings.

Miscellaneous Itemized Deductions

Certain miscellaneous expenses, mostly those related to employment, including job search expenses, and investments (other than investment-related casualty and theft losses), may be deductible only to the extent that they are above 2 percent of your AGI. For example, if your AGI is $80,000, only miscellaneous itemized deductions totaling more than $1,600 are deductible.

Therefore, it may be desirable to "bunch" these kinds of expenses to bring the total above the 2 percent floor at least every other year.

You can generally deduct (subject to the 2 percent floor) unreimbursed payments made in a given year for:

- the cost of unreimbursed job-related education or training;
- unreimbursed business use of automobiles;
- subscriptions to business or professional publications (including payment for next year's subscription);
- membership dues in business or professional associations (including the following year's dues);
- tax preparation and planning fees; and
- investment expenses, such as investment advisory fees or a safe-deposit box.

If you receive tax preparation or investment advice or certain other financial services under a fixed-fee arrangement, you may be able to take deductions this year for payments covering a period that extends into next year. Of course, if you are delaying your deductions, you will want to make these payments after the end of 2001.

Observation: Miscellaneous itemized deductions are not deductible in the AMT computation. Therefore, the AMT is a consideration when planning any acceleration of these deductions.

If you buy and sell securities, you should familiarize yourself with the definitions of "investor" and "trader." The vast majority of individuals who buy and sell for their accounts are investors. Investors deduct their investment expenses as a miscellaneous itemized deduction, subject to the 2 percent floor and the itemized deduction phase-out at higher incomes. Traders, however, may deduct their expenses against their trading income. It's difficult to convince the IRS or the courts that you are a trader unless you do a very large volume of short-term trades.

Moving Expenses

If you relocate because of a new job or business, you may be able to deduct certain moving expenses, including the costs of transporting household goods and traveling to your new residence. For these expenses to be deductible, your new job must be at least 50 miles farther from your former residence than your former job was from your former residence.

Not deductible are premove house-hunting expenses, temporary living expenses, the cost of meals while traveling or while in temporary quarters, and the costs of selling or settling a lease on the old residence or purchasing or acquiring a lease on a new residence. Employer reimbursements of deductible moving expenses are generally excluded from the employee's gross income, and deductible expenses not reimbursed by the employer are an "above-the-line deduction" instead of an itemized deduction.

 Observation: Employers often reimburse all of their employees' moving costs, including any tax liability for moving-expense reimbursements, when an employee is moved for the employer's convenience.

Above-the-line deductions are subtracted directly from your gross income to calculate AGI. They may be claimed both by itemizers and by those who take the standard deduction.

Depending on your situation, the following ideas may provide some help in reducing your tax bill.

Idea Checklist

☐ If your employer offers flexible spending accounts for medical or dependent care expenses, use them. Flexible spending accounts allow you to pay these types of expenses with pretax dollars, offering a real savings.

- If you have self-employment income and want to deduct contributions to a Keogh retirement plan, you must establish the plan by December 31, even though you can wait until the due date of your return (including extensions) to fund it. Alternatively, you may make deductible contributions to a simplified employee pension (SEP) plan, which can be established and funded after December 31 (see Chapter 3).

- Evaluate your form of business entity. Net income from a sole proprietor business, a partnership, or an LLC may be subject to self-employment tax; however, income passed through from an S corporation is not. If you work part-time for a business in addition to your full-time job, be sure you don't fall under the "hobby loss" rules; otherwise you may not be able to take losses.

- Personal property taxes such as those required for automobile license plates or tags are deductible if they are ad valorem (that is, based on the value of the property).

- If you have children in college, consider purchasing residential property near the school and renting it to your son or daughter. By doing this, you build equity in the property and can take the tax deductions associated with a rental property as long as you charge fair market value rent (subject to the passive activity rules explained in Chapter 2).

- Business owners need to remember that they can deduct only compensation that is deemed reasonable for services they and their family members provide.

This chapter has described many tools and techniques that can help you use deductions at the end of 2001 and future years to lower your tax bills.

Our next chapter sets forth a tax planning strategy called income deferral. This can be an important part of your overall tax planning program designed to maximize income and minimize taxes.

9

Deferring Income

Is it better to earn more money and pay more taxes, or earn less and pay less tax? Our own answer is simple enough: Do whatever nets more money. To that end, a taxpayer is generally well advised to brake his or her taxable income every December and postpone getting paid until the new year begins. The 2001 Tax Act makes income deferral even more valuable because income tax rates will be reduced in future years; so income deferred to a subsequent year will be taxed at lower rates, resulting in a lower overall tax bill. In addition, postponing income will delay tax liability for that income—tax will be due in the subsequent year.

Deferring income from one year to the next can be a very effective tax planning strategy, especially for those in high tax brackets because they will save the most. For tax purposes, many two-income families who may consider themselves solidly middle-class qualify as higher-income individuals. Almost all individuals report their income and deductions using the cash method of accounting (in which income is reported in the year it is actually or constructively received and expenses are deducted in the year they are paid), which gives quite a bit of flexibility in using tax-deferral strategies.

The key to saving from income deferral is that income is not taxed until it is actually or constructively received. For example, if a taxpayer does work for others, he or she will not be taxed until the year in which payment is received. So, deferring billing at year-end will result in more income being received and taxed in the following year.

What follows are some examples of situations in which income deferral may be useful.

Year-End Bonuses

If you expect to receive a year-end bonus or other special type of lump-sum compensation payment, you may want to receive it and pay taxes on it in 2002 rather than in 2001. Your employer can probably still deduct the bonus this year if the company is on the accrual method of accounting (which most larger companies are), as long as its obligation to pay you is established before year-end and payment occurs within 2½ months after year-end (March 15, 2002, for a calendar-year company).

Example: The company where you work uses the accrual accounting method, is on a calendar year, and has an incentive bonus program for which you qualify. In December 2001, the company's directors declare the bonus and set the amount of the payments, which will be paid on January 30, 2002. The result is that the company "accrues" its deduction in 2001, when it becomes liable for payment of the bonuses, but your tax liability is delayed until 2002.

Caution: This strategy of delaying payment of bonuses to the next year does not work for most payments to company owners: The company's deduction for payments to partners, S corporation shareholders, owner-employees of personal-service corporations, or shareholders who own more than 50 percent of a regular corporation is deferred until the year the bonus is actually paid to the owner—so the company is unable to accrue its deduction for the year in which the bonus was declared if it is not paid until the next year.

Deferred Compensation

You may want to consider an agreement with your employer so that part of your earnings for this year are paid to you in the future, perhaps over several years. This will delay your tax obligation and reduce the tax rate on the income because future tax rates will drop over the next few years. If you can wait until you are retired to receive the deferred compensation, you may be in a lower tax bracket, further reducing your tax bill on that income. With this type of arrangement, interest is often added by the company to compensate you for the delay in receiving the money.

The postponed compensation will not be taxed to you or be deductible by your employer until you actually receive it. But Social Security tax and Medicare tax are generally due when the income is earned. If you are already over the FICA wage base for the year ($80,400 for 2001), you won't owe any additional Social Security tax, but you and your employer will each owe the 1.45 percent Medicare tax on the deferred amount. No additional Social Security tax or Medicare tax will be owed in the future when you receive the deferred compensation.

Unlike a qualified retirement plan, which generally must cover a broad range of employees, this nonqualified type of deferred compensation arrangement can usually be made for an individual employee. If you are interested in a deferred compensation plan, you should discuss it with your employer without delay, because such a plan can only cover income you earn in the future, not that which you have already earned.

Caution: When you defer compensation, you are treated as a general creditor of your employer. If your employer goes into bankruptcy, you could lose your deferred compensation.

Stock Options or Stock Appreciation Rights

If you have nonqualified stock options or stock appreciation rights, in most cases you will have taxable compensation income when you exercise them. Delay exercising them until next year if postponing income would be to your advantage.

If you have incentive stock options, exercising them does not result in compensation income if the ISO stock is held for required periods of time (at least two years after option grant and one year after exercise). If you meet these requirements, you won't owe any tax until you sell the option stock, and then your gain is taxed at favorable capital gains rates. But the spread between the option price and the fair market value at the time you exercise the option is added to your income for AMT purposes. (See Chapter 10 for a discussion of ISOs.)

Caution: If you are a "corporate insider" as defined under Securities and Exchange Commission rules, you should contact your financial and/or legal adviser, because you are subject to special limitations on the sale of your option stock. (See Chapter 2 for more details on stock options.)

Treasury Bills and Bank Certificates

If you invest in short-term securities, you can shift interest income into the next year by buying Treasury bills or certain bank certificates with a term of one year or less that will mature next year. If you buy a bank certificate, you must specify that interest be credited only at maturity.

Dividends

If you have a voice in the management of a company in which you own stock, you may want to take steps to see that dividends are paid in January 2002 rather than in late 2001. This will shift your tax liability on the dividends to 2002, since you won't receive the dividend income until the later year.

Installment Sales

You generally owe tax on profits from the sale of property in the year in which you receive the sale proceeds. To defer income from a sale of property, consider an installment sale, in which part or all of the proceeds are payable in the following year or later. In that case, tax will be owed as you receive the payments. Part of each payment you receive will be a tax-free return of your cost or basis, part will be interest taxed at regular income tax rates, and part will be capital gain. Make sure that future payments are secured and that interest is paid on any unpaid balance.

 Caution: If the property being sold has been depreciated, usually some of the gain will be taxed, or "recaptured," at regular income tax rates. This recapture gain is subject to tax in the year of sale, even if you elect installment reporting. That is true even if you don't receive any payment in the sale year. So be sure to get enough up-front cash to at least cover your tax liability on recaptured income.

You need not decide to report 2001 deferred payment sales on the installment method until you file your 2001 tax return (in 2002). This gives you more time to decide whether to be taxed on profits in 2001 or in 2002 and later years. Note that if you choose not to report on the installment method, you must elect out of it. Also, if you do elect out, you could be liable for tax on income that you will not receive until later years.

> **Caution:** Special rules limit the use of the installment method. For example, inventory items and publicly traded stock do not qualify for installment-sale reporting. Also, installment notes in excess of $5 million may be subject to an interest charge by the IRS.

U.S. Savings Bonds

Many people are aware that the interest earned on series EE U.S. savings bonds is tax deferred for up to 30 years. However, most people are not familiar with their newer "cousins"—series I U.S. savings bonds. Series I bonds provide the same tax deferral opportunities as series EE bonds. The major difference between these two bonds is the way the interest is calculated. Series I bonds pay an interest rate that is indexed for inflation.

> **Observation:** The series I bonds are one of a very limited number of investments whose return is guaranteed to keep pace with inflation. Both EE and I bonds can be bought at your bank in various denominations. Each type of bond is limited to $30,000 per person, per year.

Annuities

You can defer current investment income you now earn, such as stock dividends, bond interest, and interest on savings and money-market accounts, by transferring the funds into deferred annuities, which shelter current earnings from tax. You won't owe tax on a deferred annuity until pay-outs begin. However, to get this benefit, you generally have to tie up your funds until you are at least 59½. Similar to IRAs, deferred annuities will incur a penalty tax on premature withdrawals, subject to certain exceptions.

Individual Retirement Accounts

If you earn compensation or self-employment income, you can establish a Roth IRA or a regular IRA, assuming you meet income requirements. (See Chapter 3 for more information about IRAs.) Although your income level may disqualify you from getting the maximum benefits from these savings vehicles, you may still find some limited advantages. For example, even though you may not be able to deduct contributions to a regular IRA or qualify for the potential tax exemption of a Roth IRA, you may make nondeductible contributions to a traditional IRA no matter how high your income is and benefit from tax deferred earnings until you withdraw your money, usually at retirement.

401(k) Plans

401(k) plans are qualified retirement plans established by an employer under which employees can defer up to $10,500 of their compensation income in 2001 or $11,000 (or higher for those age 50 or older) in 2002. As with an IRA, the earnings are not taxed until withdrawn. Contributions to these plans are made on a pretax basis, meaning that you aren't currently hit with income tax on the amount you contribute. That makes it easier for you to put more money into your account. (Social Security taxes, however, are owed on amounts you elect to defer to your 401(k) account.) Also, many employers match a portion of employee deferrals. Many 401(k) plans allow you to borrow from your accounts before retirement, if the loan is repaid on a regular schedule. (See Chapter 3 for further discussion of 401(k) plans.)

Shifting Income to Family Members

Shifting income to children or other family members in lower tax brackets is an excellent long-term planning strategy for higher-income individuals. As a general rule, family income shifting should be done early in the year to get the most tax savings. It is never too early to begin planning for 2002 and later years.

Children age 14 or older are taxed at single individual tax rates (a maximum of 15 percent on the first $27,050 of taxable income in 2001; $27,950 in 2002). Also, in 2002, dependents age 14 or older will be able to benefit from the new 10 percent tax rate that will apply to their first $6,000 of taxable income. You can also shift capital gains income from your 20 percent capital gains tax rate into a child's lower 10 percent rate, or even an 8 percent rate for a five-year gain (see Chapter 2).

The issue of who actually controls the funds—you or your child or grandchild—can determine the success of strategies that seek to use a child's lower tax rate. If you keep too much control over the transferred asset, the IRS may say you really haven't transferred it for tax purposes, and will tax you on its income or sale.

The easiest way to effectively shift income is to use a custodial account, either a Uniform Gift to Minors Act (UGMA)—or Uniform Transfers to Minors Act (UTMA) account. Keep in mind that state laws typically give the child access to UGMA/UTMA funds at age 18 or 21.

Observation: A few states, such as Alaska, California, and Nevada, allow these accounts to continue to age 25 under certain circumstances, as opposed to the cutoffs at 18 or 21 in most other states.

If you want to limit your child's access to the transferred assets beyond what an UGMA/UTMA account permits, consider a trust. But be wary of trust tax brackets. For 2001, the 15 percent bracket stops at $1,800 of taxable income ($1,850 in 2002), and the top bracket starts at $8,900 of taxable income in 2001 ($9,200 in 2002). Also, trusts won't qualify for the 10 percent tax rate that begins for individuals in 2002.

If you are planning to shift income to children under age 14, keep in mind that a kiddie tax is imposed on their unearned income (such as interest, dividends, and capital gains) over $1,500 in 2001 or 2002. This income is taxable to the child at the highest tax rate of his or her parents. However, there are techniques that you can use to shift income to your children and avoid the kiddie tax.

You are permitted to shift enough assets to a child under the age of 14 to produce up to $1,500 of total 2001 or 2002 unearned income. The first $750 of that unearned income will be offset by the child's standard deduction, and the next $750 is taxed at the child's 15 percent rate. Starting in 2002, the amount taxed at the child's rate will be taxed at only 10 percent.

Example: A six-year-old child has $1,900 of interest income in 2001 and no earned income. His or her 2001 standard deduction of $750 is allocated against his or her unearned income, and the remaining net unearned income is $1,150. The first $750 of the remaining $1,150 is taxed at the child's tax rate. The remaining $400 is taxed at the parents' top tax rate.

Unearned income	$1,900
Less: Child's standard deduction	(750)
Remaining unearned income	1,150
Less: Amount taxed at child's rate	(750)
Remaining taxed at parents' top tax rate	$ 400

Observation: A transfer of assets that produces $1,500 of income to a child under the age of 14 can save a family in the 39.1 percent tax bracket almost $475. When interest rates and investment rates of return are low, transfers of substantial assets can be made without going over the $1,500 unearned income limit. Note that asset transfers should be coordinated with the gift tax rules. (See Chapter 6 for a discussion of this strategy.)

Another technique is to transfer assets that generate little or no current taxable income. For example, consider giving a child under the age of 14:

- growth stocks or growth-stock mutual fund shares;
- U.S. series EE and series I savings bonds (the interest on which may be tax deferred);

- tax deferral products, such as annuities and variable life insurance contracts;
- closely held stock of a C corporation.

These assets can be converted into investments that produce currently taxable income after the child is age 14, because income and any capital gains recognized on the conversion will be taxable at the child's tax rate, usually 15 percent for ordinary income (10 percent on the first $6,000 of taxable income in 2002) and 10 percent for long-term capital gains—8 percent for five-year gains.

Caution: Savings bonds held in your name may qualify for tax-free treatment when used to pay for your child's college education. If you transfer these bonds to your children, this exclusion will be lost. Because of income limitations on this tax-free treatment of savings bonds, however, it is not available to most middle-income and high-income individuals. Even if loss of the education tax break isn't a factor for you, it is still a good idea to purchase new savings bonds for children rather than transferring your own bonds to them. That's because you would be taxed on the bond's accrued interest as of the transfer date. So unless the bonds are very new and the accrued interest amount is small, it is better to start with new bonds in the child's name.

Our next chapter moves away from planning suggestions and techniques. It takes a close-up view of the book's bedrock concepts. Understanding these commonly used words and phrases is critical to making the best use of the tax planning strategies and tools discussed in this book.

A NUTS-AND-BOLTS
REVIEW

Basic Tax Concepts

Tax planning is a difficult, time-consuming activity at best. Fortunately, any taxpayer who gets through this book is likely to have learned a great deal about effective tax planning. The following section comprises definitions of key tax terms. These definitions, which are really a combination of glossary, encyclopedia, and FAQs, constitute an indispensable reference source for taxpayers.

The previous few chapters have described things you may be able to do at the end of the year to reduce your tax bill. At the end of this chapter, you will find valuable suggestions for steps you can take in January as part of your tax minimization program.

What is gross income?

Gross income includes all types of taxable income: wages and bonuses, taxable interest, dividends, state tax refunds, alimony, business income, capital gains, IRA distributions, taxable pensions and annuities, rent, partnership distributions, unemployment compensation, and taxable Social Security benefits.

What is adjusted gross income (AGI)?

Adjusted gross income is your gross income less certain "above the line" deductions. These deductions include:

- deductible IRA contributions (see Chapter 3);
- medical savings account contributions;
- employment-related moving expenses (see Chapter 8);
- one-half of self-employment tax;
- 60 percent (70 percent for 2002) of health insurance premiums paid by self-employeds (see Chapter 8);
- Keogh and SEP contributions for self-employeds (see Chapter 3);
- penalties on early withdrawals of savings;
- student loan interest; and
- alimony paid.

Your AGI affects the extent to which you can deduct medical expenses, casualty and theft losses, charitable contributions, and other miscellaneous items. At higher levels of AGI, your ability to benefit from some additional itemized deductions and personal exemptions is reduced or eliminated (the 2001 Tax Act starts to decrease this hidden tax rate increase in 2006).

Some tax breaks are geared to "modified" AGI, or MAGI.
What is MAGI?

A number of tax breaks are reduced or eliminated as modified adjusted gross income (MAGI) exceeds certain levels. These include the adoption credit, the exclusion for employer-provided adoption assistance, the exclusion for interest on savings bonds used for higher education, IRA deductions, Education IRAs, Roth IRAs, higher-education tax credits, the child credit, and the student-loan interest deduction.

MAGI is generally higher than adjusted gross income. That's because various tax breaks that normally reduce AGI are disallowed in figuring MAGI under the different definitions.

What is the difference between
a tax credit and a deduction?

Tax credits are more valuable than tax deductions because they lower your tax liability dollar for dollar.

A $100 tax credit reduces your taxes by a full $100. Examples of tax credits are the HOPE Scholarship and Lifetime Learning tax credits, the child credit, the child care and dependent care credits, the adoption credit, and the foreign-tax credit.

A tax deduction reduces your taxes by the amount of your expenses multiplied by your marginal tax rate. The lower your tax rate, the smaller your tax benefit from a deduction. In the 39.1 percent tax bracket, a $100 tax deduction lowers your taxes by $39.10. In the 15 percent bracket, that same $100 deduction reduces your taxes by only $15.

Observation: It is unwise to pursue tax deductions by spending money on deductible items merely to cut your tax bill. You have to lay out more money than you will save in taxes. Keep in mind that a tax deduction is of real value only if it reduces the after-tax cost of an expenditure that you would make even if it were not deductible.

How do I calculate taxable income?

Taxable income is the amount of income on which you actually pay tax. It is calculated by adding your income from all sources and subtracting allowable deductions and exemptions.

Taxable Income Computation

Income:

Wages	$350,000
Interest, Dividends, and Capital Gains	26,000
Business Income and Rental Real Estate Income	5,000
Other Income	4,500
Total Income	$385,500

Adjustments to Income:

Moving Expenses	(3,500)
Alimony	(60,000)
Total Adjustments to Income	$ (63,500)
Adjusted Gross Income	$322,000
Itemized Deductions (after phase-out applied)	(6,000)
Exemption (phased out due to income level)	none
Taxable Income	$316,000

How does marital status affect tax liability?

Your marital status on the last day of the year determines which of the four tax rate schedules applies. If you were single for most of the year but marry on December 31, the tax law treats you as married for the entire year.

Changes in marital status can affect year-end planning. Two individuals with substantial incomes who plan to get married in 2002 might benefit from accelerating income into 2001 to avoid the so-called marriage penalty (see page 275) on that income.

Widows and widowers are allowed to file a joint return with their deceased spouse in the year of the spouse's death, and to use joint-return rates for up to two additional years if they have a qualifying dependent. Widows or widowers who may be eligible to use the more favorable married filing jointly rates in 2001, but not in 2002, could benefit from accelerating income into the earlier year.

2001 Tax Rates and Projected 2002 Tax Rates

Single Individuals

Taxable Income	2002 Tax	Marginal Tax	Taxable Income	2001 Tax	Marginal Tax	Effective Tax Rate
$0	$0	10%	–	–	–	–
6,000	600	15	$0	$0	15%	0%
27,950	3,893	27	27,050	4,058	27.5	15
67,700	14,625	30	65,550	14,645	30.5	22.3
141,250	36,690	35	136,750	36,361	35.5	26.6
over 307,050	94,720	38.6	over 297,350	94,374	39.1	31.7

Married Filing Jointly

Taxable Income	2002 Tax	Marginal Tax	Taxable Income	2001 Tax	Marginal Tax	Effective Tax Rate
$0	$0	10%	–	–	–	–
12,000	1,200	15	$0	$0	15%	0%
46,700	6,405	27	45,200	6,780	27.5	15
112,850	24,265	30	109,250	24,394	30.5	22.3
171,950	41,996	35	166,500	41,855	35.5	25.1
over 307,050	89,281	38.6	over 297,350	88,307	39.1	29.7

What is the difference between marginal and effective tax rates?

"Marginal tax" is the tax on the next dollar. "Effective tax" is the average tax rate on all of your income. For example, assume that you are married, filing a joint return, and receive:

Taxable Income	$300,000
Bonus	50,000
Total Taxable Income	$350,000

The bonus is taxed at 39.1 percent. You would pay $19,550 ($50,000 x 39.1 percent) in taxes on that bonus. The 39.1 percent is your marginal tax rate.

Your marginal tax rate also determines the tax benefit of a deductible expense. For example, if you were in the 27.5 percent bracket and had $5,000 of medical expenses in excess of 7.5 percent of your AGI, which you claimed as an itemized deduction, you would reduce your taxable income by $5,000, saving $1,375 in tax dollars ($5,000 x 27.5 percent).

Caution: Your marginal tax rate is less determinative of the tax benefit of a deductible expense if your income is above about $133,000 (about $137,000 for 2002), since at that income level you begin losing some of the benefit of your itemized deductions.

Your effective tax rate is the average rate at which all of your income is taxed. To determine this rate, divide your tax liability by your taxable income. If your 2001 taxable income on a joint return is $150,000 and the amount of tax due is $36,823, your marginal rate is 30.5 percent, but your effective tax rate is only 24.5 percent ($36,823/$150,000 = 0.2455).

How do high levels of income and itemized deductions and personal exemptions affect my marginal tax rate?

For 2001, higher-income individuals are faced with statutory marginal tax rates of 30.5 percent, 35.5 percent, and 39.1 percent. Marginal rates are even higher, however, if your AGI exceeds certain levels. This is because most itemized deductions are reduced by 3 percent of AGI in excess of set income thresholds (but you can't lose more than 80 percent of your deductions), and personal exemptions phase out or are eliminated at certain income levels. See the following charts for 2001 deductions and exemptions and 2002 projected thresholds.

2001 Itemized Deduction and Personal Exemptions

Single	Married Joint	Separate	Head of Household

Standard Deductions

Regular standard deduction

$4,550	$7,600	$3,800	$6,650

Additional standard deduction
  (elderly and/or blind taxpayers)

$1,100	$900	$900	$1,100

Kiddie tax deduction

$750	$750	$750	$750

Itemized Deduction Phase-Out
  Deductions reduced for AGI exceeding

$132,950	$132,950	$66,475	$132,950

Personal Exemption
  Each person

$2,900	$2,900	$2,900	$2,900

Personal Exemption Phase-Out
  Exemptions reduced for AGI exceeding

$132,950	$199,450	$99,725	$166,200

2002 Itemized Deduction and Personal Exemptions (Projected)

Single	Married Joint	Separate	Head of Household
Standard Deductions			
Regular standard deduction			
$4,700	$7,850	$3,925	$6,900
Additional standard deduction (elderly and/or blind taxpayers)			
$1,150	$900	$900	$1,150
Kiddie tax deduction			
$750	$750	$750	$750
Itemized Deduction Phase-Out *Deductions reduced for AGI exceeding*			
$137,300	$137,300	$68,650	$137,300
Personal Exemption *Each person*			
$3,000	$3,000	$3,000	$3,000
Personal Exemption Phase-Out *Exemptions reduced for AGI exceeding*			
$137,300	$206,000	$103,000	$171,650

The existing rules reducing itemized deductions allow you to claim at least 20 percent of your deductions regardless of your income level. Also, this limit does not affect deductions for medical expenses, casualty losses, and investment interest.

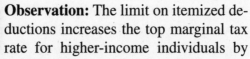

Observation: The limit on itemized deductions increases the top marginal tax rate for higher-income individuals by 1.17 percent. The phase-out of personal exemptions increases the top marginal tax rate for these families and individuals by approximately 0.75 percent for income in the phase-out range for each exemption claimed.

What is the practical result of itemized deductions limit and personal exemptions phase-out?

Higher-income individuals can end up paying federal taxes at a marginal rate of about 42 percent. For a family of four, the rate could be 45 percent, and higher if more personal exemptions are claimed. If state and local income taxes are taken into account, marginal tax rates can exceed 50 percent.

Observation: The 2001 Tax Act will start to eliminate the phase-outs of itemized deductions and personal exemptions beginning in 2006.

How are Social Security taxes figured?

If you are employed, you are subject to a 7.65 percent tax rate (6.2 percent for Social Security and 1.45

percent for Medicare). Your employer also pays the same rates to the government. If you are self-employed, you pay a 15.3 percent self-employment tax (12.4 percent for Social Security and 2.9 percent for Medicare). Self-employeds are entitled to deduct one-half of their self-employment tax. The maximum annual earnings subject to the Social Security tax are $80,400 in 2001. This amount will increase for 2002. All earnings are subject to the Medicare portion of the tax.

If you work while collecting Social Security benefits and are age 62 through 64, your benefits are reduced by $1 for every $2 that you earn above $10,680 in 2001 ($890 per month). This limit will increase for 2002. In the year you turn age 65, you lose $1 for every $3 of earnings above $25,000 ($2,084 per month) in 2001 ($30,000, or $2,500 per month, if you turn 65 in 2002). In the year you turn 65, the earnings limit applies only to the months before your 65th birthday. If you are 65 or older, earnings do not cause a reduction in your benefits.

If you work while collecting benefits, you also should consider that your earnings will be subject to income tax and payroll taxes, and these earnings also may subject some of your Social Security benefits to income tax. If your AGI plus half of your Social Security benefits plus your tax-exempt interest equals more than $25,000 if you're single or $32,000 if married, half of the excess amount up to half of your benefits is taxable. If your specially figured income exceeds $34,000 if single or $44,000 if married, up to 85 percent of your benefits may be subject to income tax.

What is the marriage penalty?

The marriage penalty results because the marginal tax rate is higher for married couples than it is for two single individuals with the same total income. For example, two single persons, each with taxable income of $100,000 in 2001, will each be taxed at the 30.5 percent marginal rate. If these two people are married, $38,550 of their total taxable income in 2001 (the amount above the $166,500 threshold) will be taxed at the 35.5 percent rate. Total tax for the two singles: $50,305. As a married couple, the 2001 tax would jump to $53,748.

If, however, one spouse has a much higher income than the other, there may be a marriage bonus. For example, a single person with $200,000 of taxable income in 2001 pays tax at a 35.5 percent marginal rate on $63,250 of it. If that same person were married and his or her spouse had no income, the couple would pay a marginal rate of 35.5 percent on only $33,500 of the income using joint-return rates.

Some married couples may benefit by filing separately. For example, it may make sense to file separately if one spouse is in a lower tax bracket and has large medical bills. The AGI threshold limiting the deduction of these medical expenses would be lower, allowing a larger deduction.

Observation: It is important to work out the numbers before deciding what to do. Over the years, Congress has added "penalty" provisions to the Tax Code to discourage married people from filing separate returns. So filing separately may seem like a good idea for one reason or another but might result in higher taxes overall than if you file jointly.

Observation: The 2001 Tax Act takes some action to reduce the marriage penalty (see Chapter 1), but none of it applies in 2001, and the most important of the changes don't begin to take effect until 2005. So the marriage penalty is still with us and will continue to be with us, albeit to a lesser extent, even after the 2001 Tax Act changes are fully phased in by 2010.

What is an accountable plan?

Business expenses reimbursed by your employer may be included as income on your Form W-2 unless your employer reimburses under an "accountable plan." An accountable plan requires documentation before a return is filed of all advanced or reimbursed expenses and the return of any excess amounts. Expenses reimbursed under a nonaccountable plan can be included in your income and are deductible, as are unreimbursed employee business expenses, as miscellaneous itemized deductions, if you have receipts and other required substantiation.

 Observation: A nonaccountable plan is not as good as it may at first sound, because miscellaneous itemized deductions can be claimed only to the extent that they total more than 2 percent of your AGI. So if your AGI is $100,000, your first $2,000 of miscellaneous expenses are nondeductible. In addition, you would receive no tax benefits from the deduction of unreimbursed business expenses if you are subject to the Alternative Minimum Tax. The AMT is described in detail below.

What are the tax effects of alimony?

Alimony is included in the gross income of the person receiving it and is deductible by the person paying it.

 Observation: Alimony is deducted "above the line" in arriving at AGI. Therefore, it can be claimed whether you itemize your deductions or take the standard deduction.

Alimony payments are not treated as alimony for tax purposes if the spouses are still in the same household. It is also important to note that large decreases in the amount of alimony in the second and third years following a divorce trigger IRS concern that property settlement amounts, which are nondeductible, are being treated as alimony. There are guidelines on what payments under a divorce or separation agreement qualify as alimony for tax purposes. For example, making rent or mortgage payments for a spouse or ex-spouse may be deductible alimony, but the value of rent-free accommodations (for example, allowing a spouse or former spouse to live without paying rent in a house you own) is not deductible.

When do I pay Social Security taxes for my domestic employees?

You must pay and withhold Social Security tax for domestic employees earning more than $1,300 during 2001. This figure will be increased for future inflation. You report this tax liability each year as a balance due on your Form 1040, Schedule H. Be sure to increase your wage withholding or make quarterly estimated payments to pay the tax associated with these employees and avoid an estimated tax underpayment penalty.

How do I figure my estimated tax payments?

The government requires estimated payments because they prefer receiving tax payments throughout the year. Individuals can have only a $1,000 or lower balance due on their tax returns to avoid an estimated tax underpayment penalty, unless certain standards are met. An interest-based underpayment of estimated tax penalty is charged if no exception applies.

In general, there are three methods that can be used to avoid an underpayment penalty:

- Estimated tax payments and/or withholding are equal to at least 100 percent of last year's tax liability. However, if your 2000 AGI exceeded $150,000, your 2001 estimated taxes must be 110 percent of your 2000 tax liability to fall within this safe harbor. And for 2002, estimated tax payments must be at least 112 percent of your 2001 tax liability to fall within it.
- 90 percent of your current-year tax liability is paid through estimated tax payments and/or withholding.
- 90 percent of annualized income (determined each quarter based on actual income) is paid through estimated tax payments and/or withholding.

These methods are applied to each quarter using one-fourth of the amounts shown above. A different one of these methods can be applied each quarter.

 Observation: The annualization method is generally best if a large part of your income is received in the latter part of the year.

Dates on Which You Must Pay Your Estimated Taxes

April 15:	Based on actual income through March 31.
June 15:	Based on actual income through May 31.
September 15:	Based on actual income through August 31.
January 15:	Based on actual income through December 31.

 Caution: If you use the "90 percent of current year's tax liability" method to calculate your estimated tax payments and recognize a large gain at year-end, you could be saddled with estimated tax penalties from a shortfall in earlier payments. So, if you have a choice as to when you recognize the gain, remember to consider estimated taxes.

 Observation: If you fall behind in estimated tax installments at the beginning of a year, you may avoid or reduce an estimated tax penalty by having additional tax withheld from your wages during the latter part of the year. Wage withholding is treated as occurring evenly over the course of the year, so one-quarter of each dollar withheld is treated as having been withheld in each quarter of the year.

You can make additional payments at any time during the year to reduce or, in some cases, eliminate potential estimated tax underpayments. Be careful not to overpay, though, because the excess payment is essentially an interest-free loan to the government.

 Observation: Use of either the annualization method or the 90 percent of current year's tax liability method is a good idea if your year-over-year income decreases or increases from one year to the next by only a small amount. But if you have a sizable increase in income (for instance, if 100 percent [or 110 percent or 112 percent for those with an AGI over $150,000] of your prior year's tax will be less than 90 percent of the tax due on your current year's income), using the "percentage of the prior year's tax liability" method allows the payment of lower estimated tax; this method is also far simpler, because you are using actual numbers, not estimates.

What is the Alternative Minimum Tax?

The Alternative Minimum Tax (AMT) was designed to ensure that every individual and corporation pays at least some tax every year. In practice, the AMT is a separate tax system that runs alongside the regular tax system. It includes a broader base of income and a smaller range of allowable deductions and credits. If you have many so-called preference items or adjustments (certain deductions and tax credits), you may have to figure and pay your tax under the AMT system. If the AMT applies and your regular taxable income is fairly small, consider gearing year-end planning toward reducing the AMT rather than regular tax.

The AMT is a two-tier system. Individuals with AMT income (AMTI) up to $175,000 (or $87,500 for married filing separately) over the exemption amount are subject to a 26 percent tax rate. A 28 percent tax rate applies to AMTI above these amounts.

The exemption amounts are:

- $49,000—Married filing jointly or surviving spouses
- $35,750—Single or head of household
- $24,500—Married filing separately

The AMT exemption amount phases out for higher-income individuals. For married individuals filing jointly or surviving spouses, the phase-out begins at AMTI of $150,000 and ends at $346,000. For single or head of household, the phase-out range is $112,500–$255,500. For married filing separately, the phase-out range is $75,000–$173,000. Married persons who file separate returns not only lose their exemptions when AMTI reaches $173,000, but must increase AMTI by 25 percent of the amount by which it exceeds $173,000 up to an overall increase of $24,500 to bring them in parity with married individuals filing jointly.

Caution: The 2001 Tax Act increased the AMT exemption amounts to the above levels, but only for 2001 through 2004. If Congress doesn't take additional action, the exemption amounts will drop back to the 2000 level in 2005. That would subject many more people to the AMT.

 Observation: Because the regular tax brackets are indexed for inflation, but the AMT tax brackets are not, many more individuals will be subject to the AMT unless Congress adjusts the AMT brackets.

 Observation: Don't think that the AMT hits only wealthy tax-shelter investors. Some of the items that lower your regular taxes but not your AMT might surprise you: State and local income taxes, property taxes, personal exemptions, home-equity-debt interest, some medical expenses, and even the standard deduction are not allowed for AMT purposes. If you're from a high-tax state and have a large family, you may be subject to the AMT.

If possible, consider spreading preference items over two or more years to take advantage of AMT exemption amounts and the 26 percent first-tier AMT rate.

Calculating AMT

In general, the AMT is calculated as follows:

1. Begin with regular taxable income.
2. Add any personal exemption amounts claimed.
3. Add any net operating loss.
4. Subtract itemized deductions that cannot be claimed on Schedule A because of certain limits for high-income individuals.
5. Adjust taxable income for certain deductions and preference items, including any AMT net operating losses to arrive at AMTI.
6. Subtract the AMT exemption amount.
7. Multiply by the AMT rate.
8. Subtract AMT credits.
9. Compare with regular tax and pay AMT to the extent it exceeds regular tax.

The AMT may increase your tax bill if you have one or more of the following items and they are sizable in relation to your total taxable income:

• itemized deductions, especially state and local income taxes, real property taxes (for example, the taxes you pay on your home and other real estate you own), certain interest, and miscellaneous itemized deductions;

- a large number of dependents;
- accelerated depreciation;
- interest income on certain tax-exempt private activity bonds issued after August 7, 1986;
- large bargain elements (spread between the option price and the fair market value of the stock at the time of exercise) on exercise of incentive stock options;
- certain deductions generated in oil, gas, or other natural resources business operations;
- large long-term capital gains.

The following example provides some of the more common adjustments and preferences that may subject a typical married couple to AMT.

Alternative Minimum Tax Calculation

Part I: Adjustments and Preferences

Medical and dental expenses allowed on Schedule A (lesser of medical and dental expenses allowed on Schedule A or 2½% of AGI)	$0
Taxes (state and local income tax, real estate, personal property, other taxes)	$287,000
Miscellaneous itemized deductions (after 2% floor)	5,000
Incentive stock options	$50,000
Passive activities	$95,000
Total adjustments and preferences	$ 437,000

Part II: Alternative Minimum Taxable Income

Taxable Income (after itemized deductions but before exemptions)	$1,000,000
Phased-out portion of itemized deductions	(38,000)
Total Alternative Minimum Taxable Income	$1,399,000

Part III: Exemption Amount and Alternative Minimum Tax

Exemption amount for married filing jointly (phased out completely at $346,000)	$0
Alternative Minimum Tax base	$1,399,000
Tentative minimum tax (up to $175,000 multiply by 26%; over $175,000 multiply by 28% and subtract $3,500)	388,220
Regular tax liability	368,668
Total Alternative Minimum Tax	$19,552

The couple in the above example is subject to the Alternative Minimum Tax, primarily as a result of a large estimated state tax payment made on January 15, 2001, for the sale of property in December 2000. Year-end tax planning could have avoided the imposition of the AMT. The couple could have made the estimated tax payment on or before December 31, 2000, and thus in the same year the gain was included in income.

If the AMT is triggered because you include in AMTI certain itemized deductions and other "exclusion items," such as personal exemptions, state taxes, tax-exempt interest, and depletion, you may want to defer prepayment of state taxes so that you receive more benefit from the deductions in a regular tax year.

An AMT credit, which you can claim against your regular tax liability in future years, is available to the extent that your AMT is the result of certain adjustments and preferences, including incentive stock options, accelerated depreciation, intangible drilling costs, and mining and exploration costs (the so-called deferral items). No AMT credit is available for so-called exclusion preferences that permanently avoid the payment of tax, such as certain tax-exempt interest and state and local income taxes.

Planning for the AMT is extremely complex. Decisions about whether you should accelerate or defer income or deductions depend on the mix of items that give rise to the AMT. In most cases, AMT planning seeks to accelerate your income and defer your deductions. In deciding the right strategy for you, it is essential to "run the numbers" under the regular tax and the AMT for the current year as well as for future years.

January Tax Strategy Idea Checklist

Most tax help books present year-end planning ideas. We have decided to go one step further and suggest strategies that make sense to implement as early in the year as possible. Early adoption of the ideas presented in the list below may make sense to maximize your opportunities to defer tax, generate income that is tax-free, and/or shift assets or income out of your estate.

- Contribute to an IRA. (See page 116.)
- Contribute to a Coverdell Education Savings Account. (See page 162.)
- Contribute to a Section 529 plan to the amount of the state tax deduction (if available). (See page 156.)
- Make a contribution to your Keogh. (See page 114.)
- Consider a Roth IRA conversion. (See page 120.)
- Think about making additional gifts of $325,000 if you have already fully used your unified credit of $675,000. Note that if you're in the maximum gift tax bracket you can give up to $250,500 gift tax-free. (See page 183.)
- Make payments that were due in 2001 that you deferred to 2002 because of the AMT. (See pages 216–217.)
- Purchase the annual maximum of Series I bonds. (See page 252.)
- Make $11,000 ($22,000 for married couples) annual exclusion gifts. (See page 194.)

Conclusion

Rumor has it that although some people love tax planning, most people would prefer to do almost anything else. But what most of us consider a burden needn't be a nightmare or a mystery. Our collective experience has shown us that millions can understand their tax options and intelligently choose those options best suited to their needs. This book is intended to be a liberating guide, grounded in our belief that every tax problem has a solution, if accurate and accessible information is available.

We have given readers a lot to consider. The first chapter laid out the tax changes introduced by the 2001 Tax Act, which will take effect over the next 10 years. The rest of the book provides a wide range of information and strategies and covers diverse areas, such as investments, retirement planning, home ownership, education savings, estate planning, and year-end tax planning. It also explains many basic tax concepts. The tax laws are incredibly complex. The Internal Revenue Code, along with its regulations and related cases, procedures, and rulings, can fill whole library rooms. And as difficult as the law is, specific financial, family, and business situations can complicate things further, making tax planning a highly personal and individualized undertaking.

We have offered a foundation. This book contains information and strategies that will make most individuals aware of ideas that may work for them and help them avoid costly tax mistakes. You should supplement this new foundation in taxes by considering how your personal situation plays into tax decisions. Tax planning never occurs in a vacuum, but is just a part, albeit an important part, of an overall financial planning process.

The tax strategies described in this book have been developed from the combined experience of many PricewaterhouseCoopers professionals. However, because every individual has unique circumstances, it is important that you consult a tax professional before implementing any tax strategy described in this book or elsewhere.

Richard J. Berry Jr. is a partner of PricewaterhouseCoopers and the leader of the firm's Tax and Legal Services division for the Americas—a $2 billion business employing more than 8,000 individuals. Rick has been with the firm for nearly thirty years and has served in leadership positions within the firm for twenty years. Rick is a C.P.A. He received his B.A. from Catholic University, his M.B.A. from Rutgers University, and a D.B.A. from George Washington University.

Michael B. Kennedy is a partner of PricewaterhouseCoopers and the national director of the firm's Personal Financial Services practice, which provides comprehensive financial planning services to high-net-worth individuals, corporate executives, business owners, and entrepreneurs. Michael has been with the firm for more than twenty-six years. Michael is a C.P.A. and member of the American, Pennsylvania, New Jersey, and Delaware Institutes of Certified Public Accountants. He has both a B.S. in economics and an M.B.A. from Rider University. He is a member of the board of trustees of Rider University and was most recently honored by his alma mater with a lifetime achievement award from the school of business.

Bernard S. Kent is the Midwest region partner-in-charge of Personal Financial Services for PricewaterhouseCoopers LLP. He has more than twenty-seven years of experience encompassing all phases of tax planning and personal financial counseling. He has been quoted in numerous national periodicals, including *The Wall Street Journal, Forbes, Fortune, U.S. News and World Report, Investor's Business Daily, Business Week, Kiplinger's,* and *Inc.*, and has been chosen three times by *Worth* magazine as one of the best financial advisers in the country. He is the past chairman of the personal financial planning committee of the Michigan Association of Certified Public Accountants. Bernie received his B.A. in economics from Oakland University and his J.D. from the University of Michigan law school.